George MacDonald

Epea Aptera; Unspoken Sermons

Third Serie

George MacDonald

Epea Aptera; Unspoken Sermons
Third Serie

ISBN/EAN: 9783744746670

Printed in Europe, USA, Canada, Australia, Japan

Cover: Foto ©Lupo / pixelio.de

More available books at **www.hansebooks.com**

Ἑπτὰ Ἄπτερα

UNSPOKEN SERMONS

THIRD SERIES

By GEORGE MAC DONALD

AUTHOR OF 'WITHIN AND WITHOUT,' 'THE MIRACLES OF OUR LORD,'
ETC. ETC.

Comfort ye, comfort ye my people

LONDON
LONGMANS, GREEN, AND CO.
AND NEW YORK : 15 EAST 16th STREET
1889

TO MY WIFE.

Sun and wind and rain, the Lord
 Is to seed his Father buried;
For he is the living Word,
 And the quickening Spirit.

BORDIGHERA:
 May 3, 1889.

CONTENTS.

	PAGE
THE CREATION IN CHRIST	1
THE KNOWING OF THE SON	25
THE MIRRORS OF THE LORD	42
THE TRUTH	56
FREEDOM	83
KINGSHIP	98
JUSTICE	109
LIGHT	163
THE DISPLEASURE OF JESUS	182
RIGHTEOUSNESS	209
THE FINAL UNMASKING	229
THE INHERITANCE	247

THE CREATION IN CHRIST.

> All things were made by him, and without him was not anything made that was made. In him was life, and the life was the light of men.—*John* i. 3, 4.

IT seems to me that any lover of the gospel given to thinking, and especially one accustomed to the effort of uttering thought, can hardly have failed to feel dissatisfaction, more or less definite, with the close of the third verse, as here presented to English readers. It seems to me in its feebleness, unlike, and rhetorically unworthy of the rest. That it is no worse than pleonastic, that is, redundant, therefore only unnecessary, can be no satisfaction to the man who would find perfection, if he may, in the words of him who was nearer the Lord than any other. The phrase 'that was made' seems, from its uselessness, weak even to foolishness after what precedes: 'All things were made by him, and without him was not anything made *that was made.*'

My hope was therefore great when I saw, in reading the Greek, that the shifting of a period would rid me of the pleonasm. If thereupon any precious result of meaning should follow, the change would not merely be justifiable—seeing that points are of no authority with anyone accustomed to the vagaries of scribes, editors, and printers—but one for which to give thanks to God. And I found the change did unfold such a truth as showed the rhetoric itself in accordance with the highest thought of the apostle. So glad was I, that it added little to my satisfaction to find the change supported by the best manuscripts and versions. It could add none to learn that the passage had been, in respect of the two readings, a cause of much disputation : the ground of argument on the side of the common reading, seemed to me worse than worthless.

Let us then look at the passage as I think it ought to be translated, and after that, seek the meaning for the sake of which it was written. It is a meaning indeed by no means dependent for its revelation on this passage, belonging as it does to the very truth as it is in Jesus ; but it is therein magnificently expressed by the apostle, and differently from anywhere else—that is, if I am right in the interpretation which suggested itself the moment I saw the probable rhetorical relation of the words.

'All things were made through him, and without him was made not one thing. That which was made in him was life, and the life was the light of men.'

Note the antithesis of the *through* and the *in*.

In this grand assertion seems to me to lie, more than shadowed, the germ of creation and redemption—of all the divine in its relation to all the human.

In attempting to set forth what I find in it, I write with no desire to provoke controversy, which I loathe, but with some hope of presenting to the minds of such as have become capable of seeing it, the glory of the truth of the Father and the Son, as uttered by this first of seers, after the grandest fashion of his insight. I am as indifferent to a reputation for orthodoxy as I despise the championship of novelty. To the untrue, the truth itself must seem unsound, for the light that is in them is darkness.

I believe, then, that Jesus Christ is the eternal son of the eternal father; that from the first of firstness Jesus is the son, because God is the father—a statement imperfect and unfit because an attempt of human thought to represent that which it cannot grasp, yet which it so believes that it must try to utter it even in speech that cannot be right. I believe therefore that the Father is the greater, that if the Father had not been, the Son could not have been. I will not apply logic to the thesis, nor would I state it now but for the sake of what is to follow. The true heart will remember the inadequacy of our speech, and our thought also, to the things that lie near the unknown roots of our existence. In saying what I do, I only say what Paul implies when he speaks of the Lord giving up the kingdom to his father, that God may be all in all. I worship the Son as the human God, the divine, the only Man, deriving his being and power from the Father, equal with him as a son is the equal at once and the subject of his father—but *making himself the equal of his father in what is most precious in Godhead, namely, Love*—which is, indeed, the essence of that statement of the evangelist with which I have now to do—a higher thing than the making of the worlds and the things in them, which he did by the power of the Father, not by a self-existent power in himself, whence the apostle, to whom the Lord must have said things he did not say to the rest, or who was better able to receive what he said to all, says, 'All things were made' not *by*, but '*through* him.'

We must not wonder things away into nonentity, but try to present them to ourselves after what fashion we are able—our shadows of the heavenly. For our very beings and understandings and consciousnesses, though but shadows in regard to any perfection either of outline or operation, are yet shadows of his being, his understanding, his consciousness, and he has cast those shadows; they are no more causally our own than his power of creation is ours. In our shadow-speech then, and following with my shadow-understanding as best I can the words of the evangelist, I say, The Father, in bringing out of the unseen the things that are seen, made essential use of the Son, so that all that exists was created *through* him. What the difference between the part in creation of the Father and the part of the Son may be, who can understand?—but perhaps we may one day come to see into it a little; for I dare hope that, through our willed sonship, we shall come far nearer ourselves to creating. The word *creation* applied to the loftiest success of human genius, seems to me a mockery of humanity, itself in process of creation.

Let us read the text again: 'All things were made *through* him, and without him was made not one thing. That which was made *in* him was life.' You begin to see it? The power by which he created the worlds was given him by his father; he had in himself a greater power than that by which he made the worlds. There was something made, not *through* but *in* him; something brought into being by himself. Here he creates in his grand way, in himself, as did the Father. 'That which was made *in* him was *life.*'

What does this mean? What is the *life* the apostle intends? Many forms of life have come to being through the Son, but those were results, not forms of the life that was brought to existence *in* him. He could not have been employed by the Father in creating, save in virtue of the life that was *in* him.

As to what the life of God is to himself, we can only know that we cannot know it—even that not being absolute ignorance, for no one can see that, from its very nature, he cannot understand a thing, without therein approaching that thing in a most genuine manner. As to what the life of God is in relation to us, we know that it is the causing life of everything that we call life—of everything that is; and in knowing this, we know something of that life, by the very forms of its force. But the one interminable mystery, for I presume the two make but one mystery—a mystery that must be a mystery to us for ever, not because God will not explain it, but because God himself could not make us understand it—is first, how he can be self-existent, and next, how he can make other beings exist: self-existence and creation no man will ever understand. Again, regarding the matter from the side of the creature—the cause of his being is antecedent to that being; he can therefore have no knowledge of his own creation; neither could he understand that which he can do nothing like. If we could make ourselves, we should understand our creation, but to do that we must be God. And of all ideas this— that, with the self-dissatisfied, painfully circumscribed consciousness I possess, I could in any way have caused myself, is the most dismal and hopeless. Nevertheless, if I be a child of God, I must be *like* him, like him even in the matter of this creative energy. There must be something in me that corresponds in its childish way to the eternal might in him. But I am forestalling. The question now is: What was that life, the thing made *in* the Son—made by him inside himself, not outside him—made not *through* but *in* him—the life that was his own, as God's is his own?

It was, I answer, that act in him that corresponded in him, as the son, to the self-existence of his father. Now what is the deepest in God? His power? No, for power could not make him what we mean when we say *God*. Evil could, of course, never create one atom; but let us understand very plainly, that a being whose essence was only power would be such a negation of the divine that no righteous worship could be offered him: his service must be fear, and fear only. Such a being, even were he righteous in judgment, yet could not be God. The God himself whom we love could not be righteous were he not something deeper and better still than we generally mean by the word—but, alas, how little can language say without seeming to say something wrong! In one word, God is Love. Love is the deepest depth, the essence of his nature, at the root of all his being. It is not merely that he could not be God, if he had made no creatures to whom to be God; but love is the heart and hand of his creation; it is his right to create, and his power to create as well. The love that foresees creation is itself the power to create. Neither could he be righteous—that is, fair to his creatures—but that his love created them. His perfection is his love. All his divine rights rest upon his love. Ah, he is not the great monarch! The simplest peasant loving his cow, is more divine than any monarch whose monarchy is his glory. If God would not punish sin, or if he did it for anything but love, he would not be the father of Jesus Christ, the God who works as Jesus wrought.

What then, I say once more, is in Christ correspondent to the creative power of God? It must be something that comes also of love; and in the Son the love must be to the already existent. Because of that eternal love which has no beginning, the Father must have the Son. God could not love, could not be love, without making things to love: Jesus has God to love; the love of the Son is responsive to the love of the Father. The response to self-existent love is self-abnegating love. The refusal of himself is that in Jesus which corresponds to the creation of God. His love takes action, creates, in self-abjuration, in the death of self as motive; in the drowning of self in the life of God, where it lives only as love. What is life in a child? Is it not perfect response to his parents? thorough oneness with them? A child at strife with his parents, one in whom their will is not his, is no child; as a child he is dead, and his death is manifest in rigidity and contortion. His spiritual order is on the way to chaos. Disintegration has begun. Death is at work in him. See the same child yielding to the will that is righteously above his own; see the life begin to flow from the heart through the members; see the relaxing limbs; see the light rise like a fountain in his eyes, and flash from his face! Life has again its lordship!

The life of Christ is this—negatively, that he does nothing, cares for nothing for his own sake; positively, that he cares with his whole soul for the will, the pleasure of his father. Because his father is his father, therefore he will be his child. The truth in Jesus is his relation to his father; the righteousness of Jesus is his fulfilment of that relation. Meeting this relation, loving his father with his whole being, he is not merely alive as born of God; but, giving himself with perfect will to God, choosing to die to himself and live to God, he therein creates in himself a new and higher life; and, standing upon himself, has gained the power to awake life, the divine shadow of his own, in the hearts of us his brothers and sisters, who have come from the same birth-home as himself, namely, the heart of his God and our God, his father and our father, but who, without our elder brother to do it first, would never have chosen that self-abjuration which is life, never have become alive like him. To will, not from self, but with the Eternal, is to live.

This choice of his own being, in the full knowledge of what he did; this active willing to be the Son of the Father, perfect in obedience—is that in Jesus which responds and corresponds to the self-existence of God. Jesus rose at once to the height of his being, set himself down on the throne of his nature, in the act of subjecting himself to the will of the Father as his only good, the only *reason* of his existence. When he died on the cross, he did that, in the wild weather of his outlying provinces, in the torture of the body of his revelation, which he had done at home in glory and gladness. From the infinite beginning—for here I can speak only by contradictions—he completed and held fast the eternal circle of his existence in saying, 'Thy will, not mine, be done!' He made himself what he is by *deathing* himself into the will of the eternal Father, through which will he was the eternal Son—thus plunging into the fountain of his own life, the everlasting Fatherhood, and taking the Godhead of the Son. This is the life that was made *in* Jesus: 'That which was made in him was life.' This life, self-willed in Jesus, is the one thing that makes such life—the eternal life, the true life, possible—nay, imperative, essential, to every man, woman, and child, whom the Father has sent into the outer, that he may go back into the inner world, his heart. As the self-existent life of the Father has given us being, so the willed devotion of Jesus is his power to give us eternal life like his own—to enable us to do the same. There is no life for any man, other than the same kind that Jesus has; his disciple must live by the same absolute devotion of his will to the Father's; then is his life one with the life of the Father.

Because we are come out of the divine nature, which chooses to be divine, we must *choose* to be divine, to be of God, to be one with God, loving and living as he loves and lives, and so be partakers of the divine nature, or we perish. Man cannot originate this life; it must be shown him, and he must choose it. God is the father of Jesus and of us—of every possibility of our being; but while God is the father of his children, Jesus is the father of their sonship; for in him is made the life which is sonship to the Father—the recognition, namely, in fact and life, that the Father has his claim upon his sons and daughters. We are not and cannot become true sons without our will willing his will, our doing following his making. It was the will of Jesus to be the thing God willed and meant him, that made him the true son of God. He was not the son of God because he could not help it, but because he willed to be in himself the son that he was in the divine idea. So with us: we must *be* the sons we are. We are not made to be what we cannot help being; sons and daughters are not after such fashion! We are sons and daughters in God's claim; we must be sons and daughters in our will. And we can be sons and daughters, saved into the original necessity and bliss of our being, only by choosing God for the father he is, and doing his will—yielding ourselves true sons to the absolute Father. Therein lies human bliss—only and essential. The working out of this our salvation must be pain, and the handing of it down to them that are below must ever be in pain; but the eternal form of the will of God in and for us, is intensity of bliss.

'And the life was the light of men.'

The life of which I have now spoken became light to men in the appearing of him in whom it came into being. The life became light that men might see it, and themselves live by choosing that life also, by choosing so to live, such to be.

There is always something deeper than anything said—a something of which all human, all divine words, figures, pictures, motion-forms, are but the outer laminar spheres through which the central reality shines more or less plainly. Light itself is but the poor outside form of a deeper, better thing, namely, life. The life is Christ. The light too is Christ, but only the body of Christ. The life is Christ himself. The light is what we *see* and shall see in him; the life is what we may *be* in him. The life 'is a light by abundant clarity invisible;' it is the unspeakable unknown; it must become light such as men can see before men can know it. Therefore the obedient human God appeared as the obedient divine man, doing the works of his father—the things, that is, which his father did—doing them humbly before unfriendly brethren. The Son of the Father must take his own form in the substance of flesh, that he may be seen of men, and so become the light of men—not that men may have light, but that men may have life;—that, seeing what they could not originate, they may, through the life that is in them, begin to hunger after the life of which they are capable, and which is essential to their being;—that the life in them may long for him who is their life, and thirst for its own perfection, even as root and stem may thirst for the flower for whose sake, and through whose presence in them, they exist. That the child of God may become the son of God by beholding *the* Son, the life revealed in light; that the radiant heart of the Son of God may be the sunlight to his fellows; that the idea may be drawn out by the presence and drawing of the Ideal

—that Ideal, the perfect Son of the Father, was sent to his brethren.

Let us not forget that the devotion of the Son could never have been but for the devotion of the Father, who never seeks his own glory one atom more than does the Son; who is devoted to the Son, and to all his sons and daughters, with a devotion perfect and eternal, with fathomless unselfishness. The whole being and doing of Jesus on earth is the same as his being and doing from all eternity, that whereby he is the blessed son-God of the father-God; it is the shining out of that life that men might see it. It is a being like God, a doing of the will of God, a working of the works of God, therefore an unveiling of the Father in the Son, that men may know him. It is the prayer of the Son to the rest of the sons to come back to the Father, to be reconciled to the Father, to behave to the Father as he does. He seems to me to say: 'I know your father, for he is my father; I know him because I have been with him from eternity. You do not know him; I have come to you to tell you that as I am, such is he; that he is just like me, only greater and better. He only is the true, original good; I am true because I seek nothing but his will. He only is all in all; I am not all in all, but he is my father, and I am the son in whom his heart of love is satisfied. Come home with me, and sit with me on the throne of my obedience. Together we will do his will, and be glad with him, for his will is the only good. You may do with me as you please; I will not defend myself. Because I speak true, my witness is unswerving; I stand to it, come what may. If I held my face to my testimony only till danger came close, and then prayed the Father for twelve legions of angels to deliver me, that would be to say the Father would do anything for his children until it began to hurt him. I bear witness that my father is such as I. In the face of death I assert it, and dare death to disprove it. Kill me; do what you will and can against me; my father is true, and I am true in saying that he is true. Danger or hurt cannot turn me aside from this my witness. Death can only kill my body; he cannot make me his captive. Father, thy will be done! The pain will pass; it will be but for a time! Gladly will I suffer that men may know that I live, and that thou art my life. Be with me, father, that it may not be more than I can bear.'

III.

Friends, if you think anything less than this could redeem the world, or make blessed any child that God has created, you know neither the Son nor the Father.

The bond of the universe, the chain that holds it together, the one active unity, the harmony of things, the negation of difference, the reconciliation of all forms, all shows, all wandering desires, all returning loves; the fact at the root of every vision, revealing that 'love is the only good in the world,' and selfishness the one thing hateful, in the city of the living God unutterable, is the devotion of the Son to the Father. It is the life of the universe. It is not the fact that God created all things, that makes the universe a whole; but that he through whom he created them loves him perfectly, is eternally content in his father, is satisfied to be because his father is with him. It is not the fact that God is all in all, that unites the universe; it is the love of the Son to the Father. For of no onehood comes unity; there can be no oneness where there is only one. For the very beginnings of unity there must be two. Without Christ, therefore, there could be no universe. The reconciliation wrought by Jesus is not the primary source of unity, of safety to the world; that reconciliation was the necessary working out of the eternal antecedent fact, the fact making itself potent upon the rest of the family—that God and Christ are one, are father and son, the Father loving the Son as only the Father can love, the Son loving the Father as only the Son can love. The prayer of the Lord for unity between men and the Father and himself, springs from the eternal need of love. The more I regard it, the more I am lost in the wonder and glory of the thing. But for the Father and the Son, no two would care a jot the one for the other. It might be the right way for creatures to love because of mere existence, but what two creatures would ever have originated the loving? I cannot for a moment believe it would have been I. Even had I come into being as now with an inclination to love, selfishness would soon have overborne it. But if the Father loves the Son, if the very music that makes the harmony of life lies, not in the theory of love in the heart of the Father, but in the fact of it, in the burning love in the hearts of Father and Son, then glory be to the Father and to the Son, and to the spirit of both, the fatherhood of the Father meeting and blending with the sonhood of the Son, and drawing us up into the glory of their joy, to share in the thoughts of love that pass between them, in their thoughts of delight and rest in each other, in their thoughts of joy in all the little ones. The life of Jesus is the light of men, revealing to them the Father.

But light is not enough; light is for the sake of life. We too must have life in ourselves. We too must, like the Life himself, live. We can live in no way but that in which Jesus lived, in which life was made in him. That way is, to give up our life. This is the one supreme action of life possible to us for the making of life in ourselves. Christ did it of himself, and so became light to us, that we might be able to do it in ourselves, after him, and through his originating act. We must do it ourselves, I say. The help that he has given and gives, the light and the spirit-working of the Lord, the spirit, in our hearts, is all in order that we may, as we must, do it ourselves. Till then we are not alive; life is not made in us. The whole strife and labour and agony of the Son with every man, is to get him to die as he died. All preaching that aims not at this, is a building with wood and hay and stubble. If I say not with whole heart, 'My father, do with me as thou wilt, only help me against myself and for thee;' if I cannot say, 'I am thy child, the inheritor of thy spirit, thy being, a part of thyself, glorious in thee, but grown poor in me: let me be thy dog, thy horse, thy anything thou willest; let me be thine in any shape the love that is my Father may please to have me; let me be thine in any way, and my own or another's in no way but thine;'—if we cannot, fully as this, give ourselves to the Father, then we have not yet laid hold upon that for which Christ has laid hold upon us. The faith that a man may, nay, must put in God, reaches above earth and sky, stretches beyond the farthest outlying star of the creatable universe. The question is not at present, however, of removing mountains, a thing that will one day be simple to us, but of waking and rising from the dead *now*.

When a man truly and perfectly says with Jesus, and as Jesus said it, 'Thy will be done,' he closes the everlasting life-circle; the life of the Father and the Son flows through him; he is a part of the divine organism. Then is the prayer of the Lord in him fulfilled: 'I in them and thou in me, that they made be made perfect in one.' The Christ in us, is the spirit of the perfect child toward the perfect father. The Christ in us is our own true nature made blossom in us by the Lord, whose life is the light of men that it may become the life of men; for our true nature is childhood to the Father.

Friends, those of you who know, or suspect, that these things are true, let us arise and live—arise even in the darkest moments of spiritual stupidity, when hope itself sees nothing to hope for. Let us not trouble ourselves about the cause of our earthliness, except we know it to be some unrighteousness in us, but go at once to the Life. Never, never let us accept as consolation the poor suggestion, that the cause of our deadness is physical. Can it be comfort to know that this body of ours, because of the death in it, is too much for the spirit —which ought not merely to triumph over it, but to inspire it with subjection and obedience? Let us comfort ourselves in the thought of the Father and the Son. So long as there dwells harmony, so long as the Son loves the Father with all the love the Father can welcome, all is well with the little ones. God is all right—why should we mind standing in the dark for a minute outside his window? Of course we miss the *inness*, but there is a bliss of its own in waiting. What if the rain be falling, and the wind blowing; what if we stand alone, or, more painful still, have some dear one beside us, sharing our *outness*; what even if the window be not shining, because of the curtains of good inscrutable drawn across it; let us think to ourselves, or say to our friend, 'God is; Jesus is not dead; nothing can be going wrong, however it may look so to hearts unfinished in childness.' Let us say to the Lord, ' Jesus, art thou loving the Father in there? Then we out here will do his will, patiently waiting till he open the door. We shall not mind the wind or the rain much. Perhaps thou art saying to the Father, " Thy little ones need some wind and rain: their buds are hard; the flowers do not come out. I cannot get them made blessed without a little more winter-weather." Then perhaps the Father will say, " Comfort them, my son Jesus, with the memory of thy patience when thou wast missing me. Comfort them that thou wast sure of me when everything about thee seemed so unlike me, so unlike the place thou hadst left."' In a word, let us be at peace, because peace is at the heart of things—peace and utter satisfaction between the Father and the Son—in which peace they call us to share; in which peace they promise that at length, when they have their good way with us, we shall share.

Before us, then, lies a bliss unspeakable, a bliss beyond the thought or invention of man, to every child who will fall in with the perfect imagination of the Father. His imagination is one with his creative will. The thing that God imagines, that thing exists. When the created falls in with the will of him who 'loved him into being,' then all is well; thenceforward the mighty creation goes on in him upon higher and yet higher levels, in more and yet more divine airs. Thy will, O God, be done! Nought else is other than loss, than decay, than corruption. There is no life but that born of the life that the Word made in himself by doing thy will, which life is the light of men. Through that light is born the life of men—the same life in them that came first into being in Jesus. As he laid down his life, so must men lay down their lives, that as he liveth they may live also. That which was made in him was life, and the life is the light of men; and yet his own, to whom he was sent, *did not believe him.*

THE KNOWING OF THE SON.

Ye have neither heard his voice at any time, nor seen his shape. And ye have not his word abiding in you; for whom he hath sent, him ye believe not.—John v. 37, 38.

WE shall know one day just how near we come in the New Testament to the very words of the Lord. That we have them with a difference, I cannot doubt. For one thing, I do not believe he spoke in Greek. He was sent to the lost sheep of the house of Israel, and would speak their natural language, not that which, at best, they knew in secondary fashion. That the thoughts of God would come out of the heart of Jesus in anything but the mother-tongue of the simple men to whom he spoke, I cannot think. He may perhaps have spoken to the Jews of Jerusalem in Greek, for they were less simple; but at present I do not see ground to believe he did.

Again, are we bound to believe that John Boanerges, who indeed best, and in some things alone, understood him, was able, after such a lapse of years, to give us in his gospel, supposing the Lord to have spoken to his disciples in Greek, the *very* words in which he uttered the simplest profundities ever heard in the human world? I do not say he was not able; I say—Are we bound to believe he was able? When the disciples became, by the divine presence in their hearts, capable of understanding the Lord, they remembered things he had said which they had forgotten; possibly the very words in which he said them returned to their memories; but must we believe the evangelists always precisely recorded his words? The little differences between their records is answer enough. The gospel of John is the outcome of years and years of remembering, recalling, and pondering the words of the Master, one thing understood recalling another. We cannot tell of how much the memory, in best condition—that is, with God in the man— may not be capable; but I do not believe that John would have always given us the very words of the Lord, even if, as I do not think he did, he had spoken them in Greek. God has not cared that we should anywhere have assurance of his very words; and that not merely, perhaps, because of the tendency in his children to word-worship, false logic, and corruption of the truth, but because he would not have them oppressed by words, seeing that words, being human, therefore but partially capable, could not absolutely contain or express what the Lord meant, and that even he must depend for being understood upon the spirit of his disciple. Seeing it could not give life, the letter should not be throned with power to kill; it should be but the handmaid to open the door of the truth to the mind that was *of* the truth.

'Then you believe in an individual inspiration to anyone who chooses to lay claim to it!'

Yes—to everyone who claims it from God; not to everyone who claims from men the recognition of his possessing it. He who has a thing, does not need to have it recognized. If I did not believe in a special inspiration to every man who asks for the holy spirit, the good thing of God, I should have to throw aside the whole tale as an imposture; for the Lord has, according to that tale, promised such inspiration to those who ask it. If an objector has not this spirit, is not inspired with the truth, he knows nothing of the words that are spirit and life; and his objection is less worth heeding than that of a savage to the assertion of a chemist. His assent equally is but the blowing of an idle horn.

'But how is one to tell whether it be in truth the spirit of God that is speaking in a man?'

You are not called upon to tell. The question for you is whether you have the spirit of Christ yourself. The question is for you to put to yourself, the question is for you to answer to yourself: Am I alive with the life of Christ? Is his spirit dwelling in me? Everyone who desires to follow the Master has the spirit of the Master, and will receive more, that he may follow closer, nearer, in his very footsteps. He is not called upon to prove to this or that or any man that he has the light of Jesus; he has to let his light shine. It does not follow that his work is to teach others, or that he is able to speak large truths in true forms. When the strength or the joy or the pity of the truth urges him, let him speak it out and not be afraid—content to be condemned for it; comforted that if he mistake, the Lord himself will condemn him, and save him 'as by fire.' The condemnation of his fellow men will not hurt him, nor a whit the more that it be spoken in the name of Christ. If he speak true, the Lord. will say 'I sent him.' For all truth is of him; no man can see a true thing to be true but by the Lord, the spirit.

'How am I to know that a thing is true?'

By *doing* what you know to be true, and calling nothing true until you see it to be true; by shutting your mouth until the truth opens it. Are you meant to be silent? Then woe to you if you speak.

'But if I do not take the words attributed to him by the evangelists, for the certain, absolute, very words of the Master, how am I to know that they represent his truth?'

By seeing in them what corresponds to the plainest truth he speaks, and commends itself to the power that is working in you to make of you a true man; by their appeal to your power of judging what is true; by their rousing of your conscience. If they do not seem to you true, either they are not the words of the Master, or you are not true enough to understand them. Be certain of this, that, if any words that are his do not show their truth to you, you have not received his message in them; they are not yet to you the word of God, for they are not in you spirit and life. They may be the nearest to the truth that words can come; they may have served to bring many into contact with the heart of God; but for you they remain as yet sealed. If yours be a true heart, it will revere them because of the probability that they are words with the meaning of the Master behind them; to you they are the rock in the desert before Moses spoke to it. If you wait, your ignorance will not hurt you; if you presume to reason from them, you are a blind man disputing of that you never saw. To reason from a thing not understood, is to walk straight into the mire. To dare to reason of truth from words that do not show to us that they are true, is the presumption of Pharisaical hypocrisy. Only they who are not true, are capable of doing it. Humble mistake will not hurt us: the truth is there, and the Lord will see that we come to know it. We may think we know it when we have scarce a glimpse of it; but the error of a true heart will not be allowed to ruin it. Certainly that heart would not have mistaken the truth except for the untruth yet remaining in it; but he who casts out devils will cast out that devil.

In the saying before us, I see enough to enable me to believe that its words embody the mind of

Christ. If I could not say this, I should say, 'The apostle has here put on record a saying of Christ's; I have not yet been able to recognize the mind of Christ in it; therefore I conclude that I cannot have understood it, for to understand what is true is to know it true.' I have yet seen no words credibly reported as the words of Jesus, concerning which I dared to say, 'His mind is not therein, therefore the words are not his.' The mind of man can receive any word only in proportion as it is the word of Christ, and in proportion as he is one with Christ. To him who does verily receive his word, it is a power, not of argument, but of life. The words of the Lord are not for the logic that deals with words as if they were things; but for the spiritual logic that reasons from divine thought to divine thought, dealing with spiritual facts.

No thought, human or divine, can be conveyed from man to man save through the symbolism of the creation. The heavens and the earth are around us that it may be possible for us to speak of the unseen by the seen; for the outermost husk of creation has correspondence with the deepest things of the Creator. He is not a God that hideth himself, but a God who made that he might reveal;

he is consistent and one throughout. There are
things with which an enemy hath meddled; but
there are more things with which no enemy could
meddle, and by which we may speak of God. They
may not have revealed him to us, but at least when
he is revealed, they show themselves so much of
his nature, that we at once use them as spiritual
tokens in the commerce of the spirit, to help convey
to other minds what we may have seen of the unseen. Belonging to this sort of mediation are the
words of the Lord I would now look into.

'And the Father himself which hath sent me,
hath borne witness of me. Ye have neither heard
his voice at any time, nor seen his shape. And ye
have not his word abiding in you: for whom he
hath sent, him ye believe not.'

If Jesus said these words, he meant more, not
less, than lies on their surface. They cannot be
mere assertion of what everybody knew; neither
can their repetition of similar negations be tautolo-
gical. They were not intended to inform the Jews
of a fact they would not have dreamed of denying.
Who among them would say he had ever heard
God's voice, or seen his shape? John himself says
'No man hath seen God at any time.' What is

the tone of the passage? It is reproach. Then he reproaches them that they had not seen God, when no man hath seen God at any time, and Paul says no man can see him! Is there here any paradox? There cannot be the sophism: 'No man hath seen God; ye are to blame that ye have not seen God; therefore all men are to blame that they have not seen God!' If we read, 'No man hath seen God, but some men ought to have seen him,' we do not reap such hope for the race as will give the aspect of a revelation to the assurance that not one of those capable of seeing him has ever seen him!

The one utterance is of John; the other of his master: if there is any contradiction between them, of course the words of John must be thrown away. But there can hardly be contradiction, since he who says the one thing, is recorder of the other as said by his master, him to whom he belonged, whose disciple he was, whom he loved as never man loved man before.

The word *see* is used in one sense in the one statement, and in another sense in the other. In the one it means *see with the eyes*; in the other, *with the soul*. The one statement is made of all men; the other is made to certain of the Jews of

Jerusalem concerning themselves. It is true that no man hath seen God, and true that some men ought to have seen him. No man hath seen him with his bodily eyes; these Jews ought to have seen him with their spiritual eyes.

No man has ever seen God in any outward, visible, close-fitting form of his own: he is revealed in no shape save that of his son. But multitudes of men have with their mind's, or rather their heart's eye, seen more or less of God; and perhaps every man might have and ought to have seen something of him. We cannot follow God into his infinitesimal intensities of spiritual operation, any more than into the atomic life-potencies that lie deep beyond the eye of the microscope: God may be working in the heart of a savage, in a way that no wisdom of his wisest, humblest child can see, or imagine that it sees. Many who have never beheld the face of God, may yet have caught a glimpse of the hem of his garment; many who have never seen his shape, may yet have seen the vastness of his shadow; thousands who have never felt the warmth of its folds, have yet been startled by

> No face: only the sight
> Of a sweepy garment vast and white.

Some have dreamed his hand laid upon them, who never knew themselves gathered to his bosom. The reproach in the words of the Lord is the reproach of men who ought to have had an experience they had not had. Let us look a little nearer at his words.

'Ye have not heard his voice at any time,' might mean, '*Ye have never listened to his voice,*' or '*Ye have never obeyed his voice;*' but the following phrase, 'nor seen his shape,' keeps us rather to the primary sense of the word *hear*: '*The sound of his voice is unknown to you;*' '*You have never heard his voice so as to know it for his.*' 'You have not seen his shape;'—'*You do not know what he is like.*' Plainly he implies, '*You ought to know his voice; you ought to know what he is like.*' 'You have not his word abiding in you;'—'*The word that is in you from the beginning, the word of God in your conscience, you have not kept with you, it is not dwelling in you; by yourselves accepted as the witness of Moses, the scripture in which you think you have eternal life does not abide with you, is not at home in you. It comes to you and goes from you. You hear, heed not, and forget. You do not dwell with it, and brood upon it, and obey it. It finds no acquaintance in you. You are not of its kind. You are not of those to whom the word of God comes. Their ears are ready to hear; they hunger after the word of the Father.'*

On what does the Lord found this his accusation of them? What is the sign in them of their ignorance of God?—'For whom he hath sent, him ye believe not.'

'How so?' the Jews might answer. 'Have we not asked from thee a sign from heaven, and hast thou not point-blank refused it?'

The argument of the Lord was indeed of small weight with, and of little use to, those to whom it most applied, for the more it applied, the more incapable were they of seeing that it did apply; but it would be of great force upon some that stood listening, their minds more or less open to the truth, and their hearts drawn to the man before them. His argument was this: 'If ye had ever heard the Father's voice; if ye had ever known his call; if you had ever imagined him, or a God anything like him; if you had cared for his will so that his word was at home in your hearts, you would have known me when you saw me—known that I must come from him, that I must be his messenger, and would have listened to me. The least acquaintance with God, such as any true heart must have, would have made you recognize that I came from the God of whom you knew that something. You would have been capable of knowing me by the light of his word abiding in you; by the shape you had beheld however vaguely; by the likeness of my face and my voice to those of my father. You would have seen my father in me; you would have known me by the little you knew of him. The family-feeling would have been awake in you, the holy instinct of the same spirit, making you know your elder brother. That you do not know me now, as I stand here speaking to you, is that you do not know your own father, even my father; that throughout your lives you have refused to do his will, and so have not heard his voice; that you have shut your eyes from seeing him, and have thought of him only as a partisan of your ambitions. If you had loved my father, you would have known his son.' And I think he might have said, 'If even you had loved your neighbour, you would have known me, neighbour to the deepest and best in you.'

If the Lord were to appear this day in England as once in Palestine, he would not come in the halo of the painters, or with that wintry shine of effeminate beauty, of sweet weakness, in which it is their helpless custom to represent him. Neither would he probably come as carpenter, or mason, or gardener. He would come in such form and condition as might bear to the present England, Scotland, and Ireland, a relation like that which the form and condition he then came in, bore to the motley Judea, Samaria, and Galilee. If he came thus, in form altogether unlooked for, who would they be that recognized and received him? The idea involves no absurdity. He is not far from us at any moment—if the old story be indeed more than the best and strongest of the fables that possess the world. He might at any moment appear: who, I ask, would be the first to receive him? Now, as then, it would of course be the childlike in heart, the truest, the least selfish. They would not be the highest in the estimation of any church, for the childlike are not yet the many. It might not even be those that knew most about the former visit of the Master, that had pondered every word of the Greek Testament. The first to cry, 'It is the Lord!' would be neither 'good churchman' nor 'good dissenter.' It would be no one with so little of the mind of Christ as to imagine him caring about stupid outside matters. It would not be the man that holds by the mooring-ring of the letter, fast in the quay of what he calls theology, and from his rotting deck abuses the presumption of those that go down to the sea in ships—lets the wind of the spirit blow where it listeth, but never blow him out among its wonders in the deep. It would not be he who, obeying a command, does not care to see reason in the command; not he who, from very barrenness of soul, cannot receive the meaning and will of the Master, and so fails to fulfil the letter of his word, making it of none effect. It would certainly, if any, be those who were likest the Master—those, namely, that did the will of their father and his father, that built their house on the rock by hearing and doing his sayings. But are there any enough like him to know him at once by the sound of his voice, by the look of his face? There are multitudes who would at once be taken by a false Christ fashioned after their fancy, and would at once reject the Lord as a poor impostor. One thing is certain: they who first recognized him would be those that most loved righteousness and hated iniquity.

But I would not forget that there are many in whom foolish forms cover a live heart, warm toward everything human and divine; for the worst-fitting and ugliest robe may hide the loveliest form. Every covering is not a clothing. The grass clothes the fields; the glory surpassing Solomon's clothes the grass; but the traditions of the worthiest elders will not clothe any soul—how much less the traditions of the unworthy! Its true clothing must grow out of the live soul itself. Some naked souls need but the sight of truth to rush to it, as Dante says, like a wild beast to his den; others, heavily clad in the garments the scribes have left behind them, and fearful of rending that which is fit only to be trodden underfoot, right cautiously approach the truth, go round and round it like a shy horse that fears a hidden enemy. But let each be true after the fashion possible to him, and he shall have the Master's praise.

If the Lord were to appear, the many who take the common presentation of thing or person for the thing or person, could never recognize the new vision as another form of the old: the Master has been so misrepresented by such as have claimed to present him, and especially in the one eternal fact of facts

—the relation between him and his father—that it is impossible they should see any likeness. For my part, I would believe in no God rather than in such a God as is generally offered for believing in. How far those may be to blame who, righteously disgusted, cast the idea from them, nor make inquiry whether something in it may not be true, though most must be false, neither grant it any claim to investigation on the chance that some that call themselves his prophets may have taken spiritual bribes

> To mingle beauty with infirmities,
> And pure perfection with impure defeature—

how far those may be to blame, it is not my work to inquire. Some would grasp with gladness the hope that such chance might be proved a fact; others would not care to discern upon the palimpsest, covered but not obliterated, a credible tale of a perfect man revealing a perfect God: they are not true enough to desire that to be fact which would immediately demand the modelling of their lives upon a perfect idea, and the founding of their every hope upon the same.

But we all, beholding the glory of the Lord, are changed into the same image.

THE MIRRORS OF THE LORD.

But we all, with open face beholding as in a glass the glory of the Lord, are changed into the same image from glory to glory, even as by the spirit of the Lord.—II. Corinthians iii. 18.

WE may see from this passage how the apostle Paul received the Lord, and how he understands his life to be the light of men, and so their life also.

Of all writers I know, Paul seems to me the most plainly, the most determinedly practical in his writing. What has been called his mysticism is at one time the exercise of a power of seeing, as by spiritual refraction, truths that had not, perhaps have not yet, risen above the human horizon; at another, the result of a wide-eyed habit of noting the analogies and correspondences between the concentric regions of creation; it is the working of a poetic imagination divinely alive, whose part is to foresee and welcome approaching truth; to discover the same principle in things that look unlike; to embody things discovered, in forms and symbols heretofore unused, and so present to other minds the deeper truths to which those forms and symbols owe their being.

I find in Paul's writing the same artistic fault, with the same resulting difficulty, that I find in Shakspere's—a fault that, in each case, springs from the admirable fact that the man is much more than the artist—the fault of trying to say too much at once, of pouring out stintless the plethora of a soul swelling with life and its thought, through the too narrow neck of human utterance. Thence it comes that we are at times bewildered between two or more meanings, equally good in themselves, but perplexing as to the right deduction, as to the line of the thinker's reasoning. The uncertainty, however, lies always in the intellectual region, never in the practical. What Paul cares about is plain enough to the true heart, however far from plain to the man whose desire to understand goes ahead of his obedience, who starts with the notion that Paul's design was to teach a system, to explain instead of help to see God, a God that can be revealed only to childlike insight, never to keenest intellect. The energy of the apostle, like that of his master, went forth to rouse men to seek the kingdom of God over them, his righteousness in them; to dismiss the lust of possession and passing pleasure; to look upon the glory of the God and Father, and turn to him from all that he hates; to recognize the brotherhood of men, and the hideousness of what is unfair, unloving, and self-exalting. His design was not to teach any plan of salvation other than obedience to the Lord of Life. He knew nothing of the so-called Christian systems that change the glory of the perfect God into the likeness of the low intellects and dull consciences of men—a worse corruption than the representing of him in human shape. What kind of soul is it that would not choose the Apollo of light, the high-walking Hyperion, to the notion of the dull, self-cherishing monarch, the law-dispensing magistrate, or the cruel martinet, generated in the pagan arrogance of Rome, and accepted by the world in the church as the portrait of its God! Jesus Christ is the *only* likeness of the living Father.

Let us see then what Paul teaches us in this passage about the life which is the light of men. It is his form of bringing to bear upon men the truth announced by John.

When Moses came out from speaking with

God, his face was radiant; its shining was a wonder to the people, and a power upon them. But the radiance began at once to diminish and die away, as was natural, for it was not indigenous in Moses. Therefore Moses put a veil upon his face that they might not see it fade. As to whether this was right or wise, opinion may differ: it is not my business to discuss the question. When he went again into the tabernacle, he took off his veil, talked with God with open face, and again put on the veil when he came out. Paul says that the veil which obscured the face of Moses lies now upon the hearts of the Jews, so that they cannot understand him, but that when they turn to the Lord, go into the tabernacle with Moses, the veil shall be taken away, and they shall see God. Then will they understand that the glory is indeed faded upon the face of Moses, but by reason of the glory that excelleth, the glory of Jesus that overshines it. Here, after all, I can hardly help asking—Would not Moses have done better to let them see that the glory of their leader was altogether dependent on the glory within the veil, whither they were not worthy to enter? Did that veil hide Moses's face only? Did he not, however unintentionally, lay it on their hearts? Did it not cling there, and help to hide God from them, so that they could not perceive that the greater than Moses was come, and stormed at the idea that the glory of their prophet must yield? Might not the absence of that veil from his face have left them a little more able to realize that his glory was a glory that must pass, a glory whose glory was that it prepared the way for a glory that must extinguish it? Moses had put the veil for ever from his face, but they clutched it to their hearts, and it blinded them—admirable symbol of the wilful blindness of old Mosaist or modern Wesleyan, admitting no light that his Moses or his Wesley did not see, and thus losing what of the light he saw and reflected.

Paul says that the sight of the Lord will take that veil from their hearts. His light will burn it away. His presence gives liberty. Where he is, there is no more heaviness, no more bondage, no more wilderness or Mount Sinai. The Son makes free with sonship.

And now comes the passage whose import I desire to make more clear:

'But we all,' having this presence and this

liberty, 'with open face beholding as in a glass the glory of the Lord, are changed into the same image,' that of the Lord, 'from glory to glory, even as of the Lord, the spirit.'

'We need no Moses, no earthly mediator, to come between us and the light, and bring out for us a little of the glory. We go into the presence of the Son revealing the Father—into the presence of the Light of men. Our mediator is the Lord himself, the spirit of light, a mediator not sent by us to God to bring back his will, but come from God to bring us himself. We enter, like Moses, into the presence of the visible, radiant God—only how much more visible, more radiant! As Moses stood with uncovered face receiving the glory of God full upon it, so with open, with uncovered face, full in the light of the glory of God, in the place of his presence, stand we—you and I, Corinthians. It is no reflected light we see, but the glory of God shining *in*, shining out of, shining in and from the face of Christ, the glory of the Father, one with the Son. Israel saw but the fading reflection of the glory of God on the face of Moses; we see the glory itself in the face of Jesus.'

But in what follows, it seems to me that the revised version misses the meaning almost as much as the authorized, when, instead of 'beholding as in a glass,' it gives 'reflecting as a mirror.' The former is wrong; the latter is far from right. The idea, with the figure, is that of a poet, not a man of science. The poet deals with the outer show of things, which outer show is infinitely deeper in its relation to truth, as well as more practically useful, than the analysis of the man of science. Paul never thought of the mirror as reflecting, as throwing back the rays of light from its surface; he thought of it as receiving, taking into itself, the things presented to it—here, as filling its bosom with the glory it looks upon. When I see the face of my friend in a mirror, the mirror seems to hold it in itself, to surround the visage with its liquid embrace. The countenance is *there*—down there in the depth of the mirror. True, it shines radiant out of it, but it is not the shining out of it that Paul has in his thought; it is the fact—the *visual* fact, which, according to Wordsworth, the poet always seizes—of the mirror holding in it the face.

That this is the way poet or prophet—Paul was

both—would think of the thing, especially in the age of the apostle, I shall be able to make appear even more probable by directing your notice to the following passage from Dante—whose time, though so much farther from that of the apostle than our time from Dante's, was in many respects much liker Paul's than ours.

The passage is this:—Dell' Inferno: Canto xxiii. 25-27:

> E quei: 'S' io fossi d' impiombato vetro,
> L' immagine di fuor tua non trarrei
> Più tosto a me, che quella dentro impetro.'

Here Virgil, with reference to the power he had of reading the thoughts of his companion, says to Dante:

'If I were of leaded glass,'—meaning, 'If I were glass covered at the back with lead, so that I was a mirror,'—'I should not draw thy outward image to me more readily than I gain thy inner one;'—meaning, 'than now I know your thoughts.'

It seems, then, to me, that the true simple word to represent the Greek, and the most literal as well by which to translate it, is the verb *mirror*—when the sentence, so far, would run thus: 'But we all, with unveiled face, mirroring the glory of the Lord,—.'

I must now go on to unfold the idea at work in the heart of the apostle. For the mere correctness of a translation is nothing, except it bring us something deeper, or at least some fresher insight: with him who cares for the words apart from what the writer meant them to convey, I have nothing to do: he must cease to ' pass for a man ' and begin to be a man indeed, on the way to be a live soul, before I can desire his intercourse. The prophet-apostle seems to me, then, to say, 'We all, with clear vision of the Lord, mirroring in our hearts his glory, even as a mirror would take into itself his face, are thereby changed into his likeness, his glory working our glory, by the present power, in our inmost being, of the Lord, the spirit.' Our mirroring of Christ, then, is one with the presence of his spirit in us. The idea, you see, is not the reflection, the radiating of the light of Christ on others, though that were a figure lawful enough; but the taking into, and having in us, him working to the changing of us.

That the thing signified transcends the sign, outreaches the figure, is no discovery; the thing figured always belongs to a higher stratum, to which the simile serves but as a ladder; when the climber has reached it, 'he then unto the ladder turns his back.' It is but according to the law of symbol, that the thing symbolized by the mirror should have properties far beyond those of leaded glass or polished metal, seeing it is a live soul understanding that which it takes into its deeps —holding it, and conscious of what it holds. It mirrors by its will to hold in its mirror. Unlike its symbol, it can hold not merely the outward visual resemblance, but the inward likeness of the person revealed by it; it is open to the influences of that which it embraces, and is capable of active co-operation with them: the mirror and the thing mirrored are of one origin and nature, and in closest relation to each other. Paul's idea is, that when we take into our understanding, our heart, our conscience, our being, the glory of God, namely Jesus Christ as he shows himself to our eyes, our hearts, our consciences, he works upon us, and will keep working, till we are changed to the very likeness we have thus mirrored in us; for with his likeness he comes himself, and dwells in us. He will work until the same likeness is wrought out and perfected in us, the image, namely, of the humanity of God, in which image we were made at first, but which could never be developed in us except by the indwelling of the perfect likeness. By the power of Christ thus received and at home in us, we are changed—the glory in him becoming glory in us, his glory changing us to glory.

But we must beware of receiving this or any symbol *after the flesh*, beware of interpreting it in any fashion that partakes of the character of the mere physical, psychical, or spirituo-mechanical. The symbol deals with things far beyond the deepest region whence symbols can be drawn. The indwelling of Jesus in the soul of man, who shall declare! But let us note this, that the dwelling of Jesus in us is the power of the spirit of God upon us; for 'the Lord is that spirit,' and that Lord dwelling in us, we are changed 'even as from the Lord the spirit.' When we think Christ, Christ comes; when we receive his image into our spiritual mirror, he enters with it. Our thought is not cut off from his. Our open receiving thought is his door to come in. When our hearts turn to him, that is opening the door to him, that is holding up our mirror to him; then he comes in, not by our thought only, not in our idea only, but he comes himself, and of his own will—comes in as we could not take him, but as he can come and we receive him—enabled to receive by his very coming the one welcome guest of the whole universe. Thus the Lord, the spirit, becomes the soul of our souls, becomes spiritually what he always was creatively; and as our spirit informs, gives shape to our bodies, in like manner his soul informs, gives shape to our souls. In this there is nothing unnatural, nothing at conflict with our being. It is but that the deeper soul that willed and wills our souls, rises up, the infinite Life, into the Self we call *I* and *me*, but which lives immediately from him, and is his very own property and nature—unspeakably more his than ours: this deeper creative soul, working on and with his creation upon higher levels, makes the *I* and *me* more and more his, and himself more and more ours; until at length the glory of our existence flashes upon us, we face full to the sun that enlightens what it sent forth, and know ourselves alive with an infinite life, even the life of the Father; know that our existence is not the moonlight of a mere consciousness of being, but the sun-glory of a life justified by having become one with its origin, thinking and feeling with the primal Sun of life, from whom it was dropped away that it might know and bethink itself, and return to circle for ever in exultant harmony around him. Then indeed we *are*; then indeed we have life; the life of Jesus has, through light, become life in us; the glory of God in the face of Jesus, mirrored in our hearts, has made us alive; we are one with God for ever and ever.

What less than such a splendour of hope would be worthy the revelation of Jesus? Filled with the soul of their Father, men shall inherit the glory of their Father; filled with themselves, they cast him out, and rot. The company of the Lord, soul to soul, is that which saves with life, his life of God-devotion, the souls of his brethren. No other saving can save them. They must receive the Son, and through the Son the Father. What it cost the Son to get so near to us that we could say *Come in*, is the story of his life. He stands at the door and knocks, and when we open to him he comes in, and dwells with us, and we are transformed to the same image of truth and purity and heavenly childhood. Where power dwells, there is no force; where the spirit-Lord is, there is liberty. The Lord Jesus, by free, potent communion with their inmost being, will change his obedient brethren till in every thought and impulse they are good like him, unselfish, neighbourly, brotherly like him, loving the Father perfectly like him, ready to die for the truth like him, caring like him for nothing in the universe but the will of God, which is love, harmony, liberty, beauty, and joy.

I do not know if we may call this having life in ourselves; but it is the waking up, the perfecting in us of the divine life inherited from our Father in heaven, who made us in his own image, whose nature remains in us, and makes it the deepest reproach to a man that he has neither heard his voice at any time, nor seen his shape. He who would thus live must, as a mirror draws into its bosom an outward glory, receive into his 'heart of heart' the inward glory of Jesus Christ, *the Truth*.

THE TRUTH.

I am the truth.—*John* xiv. 6.

WHEN the man of the five senses talks of *truth*, he regards it but as a predicate of something historical or scientific proved a fact ; or, if he allows that, for aught he knows, there may be higher truth, yet, as he cannot obtain proof of it from without, he acts as if under no conceivable obligation to seek any other satisfaction concerning it. Whatever appeal be made to the highest region of his nature, such a one behaves as if it were the part of a wise man to pay it no heed, because it does not come within the scope of the lower powers of that nature. According to the word of *the* man, however, truth means more than fact, more than relation of facts or persons, more than loftiest abstraction of metaphysical entity—means being and life, will and action ; for he says, '*I am the truth.*'

I desire to help those whom I may to understand more of what is meant by *the truth*, not for the sake of definition, or logical discrimination, but that, when they hear the word from the mouth of the Lord, the right idea may rise in their minds; that the word may neither be to them a void sound, nor call up either a vague or false notion of what he meant by it. If he says, 'I am the truth,' it must, to say the least, be well to know what he means by the word with whose idea he identifies himself. And at once we may premise that he can mean nothing merely intellectual, such as may be set forth and left there; he means something vital, so vital that the whole of its necessary relations are subject to it, so vital that it includes everything else which, in any lower plane, may go or have gone by the same name. Let us endeavour to arrive at his meaning by a gently ascending stair.

A thing being so, the word that says it is so, is the truth. But the fact may be of no value in itself, and our knowledge of it of no value either. Of most facts it may be said that the truth concerning them is of no consequence. For instance, it cannot be in itself important whether on a certain morning I took one side of the street or the other. It may be of importance to some one to know which I took, but in itself it is of none. It would therefore be felt unfit if I said, 'It is *a truth* that I walked on the sunny side.' The correct word would be *a fact*, not *a truth*. If the question arose whether a statement concerning the thing were correct, we should still be in the region of fact or no fact; but when we come to ask whether the statement was true or false, then we are concerned with the matter as the assertion of a human being, and ascend to another plane of things. It may be of no consequence which side I was upon, or it may be of consequence to some one to know which, but it is of vital importance to the witness and to any who love him, whether or not he believes the statement he makes—whether the man himself is true or false. Concerning the thing it can be but a question of *fact*; it remains a question of fact even whether the man has or has not spoken the truth; but concerning the man it is a question of truth: he is either a pure soul, so far as this thing witnesses, or a false soul, capable and guilty of a lie. In this relation it is of no consequence whether the man spoke the fact or not; if he meant to speak the fact, he remains a true man.

Here I would anticipate so far as to say that there are *truths* as well as *facts*, and lies against truths as well as against facts. When the Pharisees said *Corban*, they lied against the truth that a man must honour his father and mother.

Let us go up now from the region of facts that seem casual, to those facts that are invariable, by us unchangeable, which therefore involve what we call *law*. It will be seen at once that the *fact* here is of more dignity, and the truth or falsehood of a statement in this region of more consequence in itself. It is a small matter whether the water in my jug was frozen on such a morning; but it is a fact of great importance that at thirty-two degrees of Fahrenheit water always freezes. We rise a step here in the nature of the facts concerned: are we come therefore into the region of truths? Is it a truth that water freezes at thirty-two degrees? I think not. There is no principle, open to us, involved in the changeless fact. The principle that lies at the root of it in the mind of God must be a truth, but to the human mind the fact is as yet only a fact. The word *truth* ought to be kept for higher things. There are those that think such facts the highest that can be known; they put therefore the highest word they know to the highest thing they know, and call the facts of nature truths;

but to me it seems that, however high you come in your generalization, however wide you make your law—including, for instance, all solidity under the law of freezing—you have not risen higher than the statement that such and such is an invariable fact. Call it a law if you will—a law of nature if you choose—that it always is so, but not a truth. It cannot be to us a truth until we descry the reason of its existence, its relation to mind and intent, yea to self-existence. Tell us why it *must* be so, and you state a truth. When we come to see that a law is such, because it is the embodiment of a certain eternal thought, beheld by us in it, a fact of the being of God, the facts of which alone are truths, then indeed it will be to us, not a law merely, but an embodied truth. A law of God's nature is a way he would have us think of him; it is a necessary truth of all being. When a law of Nature makes us see this; when we say, I understand that law; I see why it ought to be; it is just like God; then it rises, not to the dignity of a truth in itself, but to the truth of its own nature—namely, a revelation of character, nature, and will in God. It is a picture of something in God, a word that tells a fact about God, and is therefore far nearer being called a truth than anything below it. As a simple illustration: What notion should we have of the unchanging and unchangeable, without the solidity of matter? If, such as we are, we had nothing solid about us, where would be our thinking about God and truth and law?

But there is a region perhaps not so high as this from the scientific point of view, where yet the word truth may begin to be rightly applied. I believe that every fact in nature is a revelation of God, is there such as it is because God is such as he is; and I suspect that all its facts impress us so that we learn God unconsciously. True, we cannot think of any one fact thus, except as we find the soul of it—its fact of God; but from the moment when first we come into contact with the world, it is to us a revelation of God, his things seen, by which we come to know the things unseen. How should we imagine what we may of God, without the firmament over our heads, a visible sphere, yet a formless infinitude! What idea could we have of God without the sky? The truth of the sky is what it makes us feel of the God that sent it out to our eyes. If you say the sky could not but be so and such, I grant it—with God at the root of it. There is nothing for us to conceive in its stead—therefore indeed it must be so. In its discovered laws, light seems to me to be such because God is such. Its so-called laws are the waving of his garments, waving so because he is thinking and loving and walking inside them.

We are here in a region far above that commonly claimed for science, open only to the heart of the child and the childlike man and woman—a region in which the poet is among his own things, and to which he has often to go to fetch them. For things as they are, not as science deals with them, are the revelation of God to his children. I would not be misunderstood: there is no fact of science not yet incorporated in a law, no law of science that has got beyond the hypothetic and tentative, that has not in it the will of God, and therefore may not reveal God; but neither fact nor law is there for the sake of fact or law; each is but a mean to an end; in the perfected end we find the intent, and there God —not in the laws themselves, save as his means. For that same reason, human science cannot discover God; for human science is but the backward undoing of the tapestry-web of God's science, works with its back to him, and is always leaving him—his intent, that is, his perfected work—behind it, always going farther and farther away from the point where his work culminates in revelation. Doubtless it thus makes some small intellectual approach to him, but at best it can come only to his back; science will never find the face of God; while those who would reach his heart, those who, like Dante, are returning thither where they are, will find also the spring-head of his science. Analysis is well, as death is well; analysis is death, not life. It discovers a little of the way God walks to his ends, but in so doing it forgets and leaves the end itself behind. I do not say the man of science does so, but the very process of his work is such a leaving of God's ends behind. It is a following back of his footsteps, too often without appreciation of the result for which the feet took those steps. To rise from the perfected work is the swifter and loftier ascent. If the man could find out why God worked so, then he would be discovering God; but even then he would not be discovering the best and the deepest of God; for his means cannot be so great as his ends. I must make myself clearer.

Ask a man of mere science, what is the truth of

a flower: he will pull it to pieces, show you its parts, explain how they operate, how they minister each to the life of the flower; he will tell you what changes are wrought in it by scientific cultivation.; where it lives originally, where it can live; the effects upon it of another climate; what part the insects bear in its varieties—and doubtless many more facts about it. Ask the poet what is the truth of the flower, and he will answer: 'Why, the flower itself, the perfect flower, and what it cannot help saying to him who has ears to hear it.' The truth of the flower is, not the facts about it, be they correct as ideal science itself, but the shining, glowing, gladdening, patient thing throned on its stalk—the compeller of smile and tear from child and prophet. The man of science laughs at this, because he is only a man of science, and does not know what it means; but the poet and the child care as little for his laughter as the birds of God, as Dante calls the angels, for his treatise on aerostation. The children of God must always be mocked by the children of the world, whether in the church or out of it— children with sharp ears and eyes, but dull hearts. Those that hold love the only good in the world, understand and smile at the world's children, and can do very well without anything they have got to tell them. In the higher state to which their love is leading them, they will speedily outstrip the men of science, for they have that which is at the root of science, that for the revealing of which God's science exists. What shall it profit a man to know all things, and lose the bliss, the consciousness of well-being, which alone can give value to his knowledge?

God's science in the flower exists for the existence of the flower in its relation to his children. If we understand, if we are at one with, if we love the flower, we have that for which the science is there, that which alone can equip us for true search into the means and ways by which the divine idea of the flower was wrought out to be presented to us. The idea of God *is* the flower; his idea is not the botany of the flower. Its botany is but a thing of ways and means—of canvas and colour and brush in relation to the picture in the painter's brain. The mere intellect can never find out that which owes its being to the heart supreme. The relation of the intellect to that which is born of the heart is an unreal except it be a humble one. The idea of God, I repeat, is the flower. He thought it;

invented its means; sent it, a gift of himself, to the eyes and hearts of his children. When we see how they are loved by the ignorant and degraded, we may well believe the flowers have a place in the history of the world, as written for the archives of heaven, which we are yet a long way from understanding, and which science could not, to all eternity, understand, or enable to understand. Watch that child! He has found one of his silent and motionless brothers, with God's clothing upon it, God's thought in its face. In what a smile breaks out the divine understanding between them! Watch his mother when he takes it home to her—no nearer understanding it than he! It is no old association that brings those tears to her eyes, powerful in that way as are flowers, and things far inferior to flowers; it is God's thought, unrecognized as such, holding communion with her. She weeps with a delight inexplicable. It is only a daisy! only a primrose! only a pheasant-eye-narcissus! only a lily of the field! only a snowdrop! only a sweet-pea! only a brave yellow crocus! But here to her is no mere fact; here is no law of nature; here is a truth of nature, the truth of a flower—a perfect thought from the heart of God—a truth of

God!—not an intellectual truth, but a divine fact, a dim revelation, a movement of the creative soul! Who but a father could think the flowers for his little ones? We are nigh the region now in which the Lord's word is at home—'I am the truth.'

I will take an illustrative instance altogether to my mind and special purpose. What, I ask, is the truth of water? Is it that it is formed of hydrogen and oxygen?—That the chemist has now another mode of stating the *fact* of water, will not affect my illustration. His new mode will probably be one day yet more antiquated than mine is now.—Is it for the sake of the fact that hydrogen and oxygen combined form water, that the precious thing exists? Is oxygen-and-hydrogen the divine idea of water? Or has God put the two together only that man might separate and find them out? He allows his child to pull his toys to pieces; but were they made that he might pull them to pieces? He were a child not to be envied for whom his inglorious father would make toys to such an end! A school-examiner might see therein the best use of a toy, but not a father! Find for us what in the constitution of the two gases makes them fit and capable to be thus honoured in forming the lovely thing, and you will give us a revelation about more than water, namely about the God who made oxygen and hydrogen. There is no water in oxygen, no water in hydrogen: it comes bubbling fresh from the imagination of the living God, rushing from under the great white throne of the glacier. The very thought of it makes one gasp with an elemental joy no metaphysician can analyse. The water itself, that dances, and sings, and slakes the wonderful thirst—symbol and picture of that draught for which the woman of Samaria made her prayer to Jesus—this lovely thing itself, whose very wetness is a delight to every inch of the human body in its embrace—this live thing which, if I might, I would have running through my room, yea, babbling along my table--this water is its own self its own truth, and is therein a truth of God. Let him who would know the love of the maker, become sorely athirst, and drink of the brook by the way—then lift up his heart—not at that moment to the maker of oxygen and hydrogen, but to the inventor and mediator of thirst and water, that man might foresee a little of what his soul may find in God. If he become not then as a hart panting for the water-brooks, let him go back to his science and its husks: they will at last make him thirsty as the victim in the dust-tower of the Persian. As well may a man think to describe the joy of drinking by giving thirst and water for its analysis, as imagine he has revealed anything about water by resolving it into its scientific elements. Let a man go to the hillside and let the brook sing to him till he loves it, and he will find himself far nearer the fountain of truth than the triumphal car of the chemist will ever lead the shouting crew of his half-comprehending followers. He will draw from the brook the water of joyous tears, 'and worship him that made heaven, and earth, and the sea, and the fountains of waters.'

The truth *of a thing*, then, is the blossom of it, the thing it is made for, the topmost stone set on with rejoicing; truth in a man's imagination is the power to recognize this truth of a thing; and wherever, in anything that God has made, in the glory of it, be it sky or flower or human face, we see the glory of God, there a true imagination is beholding a truth of God. And now we must advance to a yet higher plane.

We have seen that the moment whatever goes by the name of truth comes into connection with man; the moment that, instead of merely mirroring itself in his intellect as a thing outside of him, it comes into contact with him as a being of action; the moment the knowledge of it affects or ought to affect his sense of duty, it becomes a thing of far nobler import; the question of truth enters upon a higher phase, looks out of a loftier window. A fact which in itself is of no value, becomes at once a matter of life and death—moral life and death, when a man has the choice, the imperative choice of being true or false concerning it. When the truth, the heart, the summit, the crown of a thing, is perceived by a man, he approaches the fountain of truth whence the thing came, and perceiving God by understanding what is, becomes more of a man, more of the being he was meant to be. In virtue of this truth perceived, he has relations with the universe undeveloped in him till then. But far higher will the doing of the least, the most insignificant duty raise him. He begins thereby to be a true man. A man may delight in the vision and glory of a truth, and not himself be true. The man whose vision is weak, but who, as far as he sees, and desirous to see farther, does the thing he sees, is a true man. If a man knows what is, and says it is not, his knowing does not make him less than a liar. The man who recognizes the truth of any human relation, and neglects the duty involved, is not a true man. The man who knows the laws of nature, and does not heed them, the more he teaches them to others, the less is he a true man. But he may obey them all and be the falsest of men, because of far higher and closer duties which he neglects. The man who takes good care of himself and none of his brother and sister, is false. A man may be a poet, aware of the highest truth of a thing, of that beauty which is the final cause of its existence; he may draw thence a notion of the creative loveliness that thought it out; he may be a man who would not tell a lie, or steal, or slander—and yet he may not be a true man, inasmuch as the essentials of manhood are not his aim: having nowise come to the flower of his own being, nowise, in his higher degree, attained the truth of *a thing*—namely, that for which he exists, the creational notion of him—neither is he striving after the same. There are relations closer than those of the facts around him, plainer than those that seem to bring the maker nigh to him, which he is failing to see, or seeing fails to acknowledge, or acknowledging fails to fulfil. Man is man only in the doing of the truth, perfect man only in the doing of the highest truth, which is the fulfilling of his relations to his origin. But he has relations with his fellow man, closer infinitely than with any of the things around him, and to many a man far plainer than his relations with God. Now the nearer is plainer that he may step on it, and rise to the higher, till then the less plain. These relations make a large part of his being, are essential to his very existence, and spring from the very facts of the origination of his being. They are the relation of thought to thought, of being to being, of duty to duty. The very nature of a man depends upon or is one with these relations. They are *truths*, and the man is a true man as he fulfils them. Fulfilling them perfectly, he is himself a *truth*, a living truth. As regarded merely by the intellect, these relations are facts of man's nature; but that they are of man's *nature* makes them truths, and the fulfilments of them are duties. He is so constituted as to understand them at first more than he can love them, with the resulting advantage of having thereby the opportunity of choosing them purely because they are true; so doing he chooses to love them, and is enabled to love them in the doing, which alone can truly reveal them to him, and make the loving of them possible. Then they cease to show themselves in the form of duties, and appear as they more truly are, absolute truths, essential realities, eternal delights. The man is a true man who chooses duty; he is a perfect man who at length never thinks of duty, who forgets the name of it. The duty of Jesus was the doing in lower forms than the perfect that which he loved perfectly, and did perfectly in the highest forms also. Thus he fulfilled all righteousness. One who went to the truth by mere impulse, would be a holy animal, not a true man. Relations, truths, duties, are shown to the man away beyond him, that he may choose them, and be a child of God, choosing righteousness like him. Hence the whole sad victorious human tale, and the glory to be revealed!

The moral philosopher who regards duties only as facts of his system; nay, even the man who regards them as truths, essential realities of his humanity, but goes no farther, is essentially a liar, a man of untruth. He is a man indeed, but not a true man. He is a man in possibility, but not a real man yet. The recognition of these things is the imperative obligation to fulfil them. Not fulfilling these relations, the man is undoing the right of his own existence, destroying his *raison d'être*, making of himself a monster, a live reason why he should not live, for nothing on those terms could ever have begun to be. His presence is a claim upon his creator for destruction.

The facts of human relation, then, are truths indeed, and of awfullest import. 'Whosoever hateth his brother is a murderer ; and ye know that no murderer hath eternal life abiding in him !' The man who lives a hunter after pleasure, not a labourer in the fields of duty, who thinks of himself as if he were alone on the earth, is in himself a lie. Instead of being the man he looks, the man he was made to be, he lives as the beasts seem to live—with this difference, I trust, that they are rising, while he, so far as lies in himself, is sinking. But he cannot be allowed to sink beyond God's reach ; hence all the holy—that is, healing—miseries that come upon him, of which he complains as so hard and unfair : they are for the compelling of the truth he will not yield—a painful suasion to be himself, to be a truth.

But suppose, for the sake of my progressive unfolding, that a man did everything required of him —fulfilled all the relations to his fellows of which I have been speaking, was toward them at least, a true man; he would yet feel, doubtless would feel it the more, that something was lacking to him—lacking to his necessary well-being. Like a live flower, he would feel that he had not yet blossomed, and could not tell what the blossom ought to be. In this direction the words of the Lord point, when he says to the youth, 'If thou wouldst be perfect.' The man whom I suppose, would feel that his existence was not yet justified to itself, that the truth of his being and nature was not yet revealed to his consciousness. He would remain unsatisfied; and the cause would be that there was in him a relation, and that the deepest, closest, and strongest, which had not yet come into live fact, which had not yet become a truth in him, toward which he was not true, whereby his being remained untrue, he was not himself, was not ripened into the divine idea, which alone can content itself. A child with a child's heart who does not even know that he has a father, yet misses him—with his whole nature, even if not with his consciousness. This relation has not yet so far begun to be fulfilled in him, as that the coming blossom should send before it patience and hope enough to enable him to live by faith without sight. When the flower begins to come, the human plant begins to rejoice in the glory of God not yet revealed, the inheritance of the saints in light ; with uplifted stem and forward-leaning bud expects the hour when the lily of God's field shall know itself alive, with God himself for its heart and its atmosphere ; the hour when God and the man shall be one, and all that God cares for shall be the man's. But again I forget my progression.

The highest truth to the intellect, the abstract truth, is the relation in which man stands to the source of his being—his will to the will whence it became a will, his love to the love that kindled his power to love, his intellect to the intellect that lighted his. If a man deal with these things only as things to be dealt with, as objects of thought, as ideas to be analysed and arranged in their due order and right relation, he treats them as facts and not as truths, and is no better, probably much the worse, for his converse with them, for he knows in a measure, and is false to all that is most worthy of his faithfulness.

But when the soul, or heart, or spirit, or what

you please to call that which is the man himself and not his body, sooner or later becomes aware that he needs some one above him, whom to obey, in whom to rest, from whom to seek deliverance from what in himself is despicable, disappointing, unworthy even of his own interest; when he is aware of an opposition in him, which is not harmony; that, while he hates it, there is yet present with him, and seeming to be himself, what sometimes he calls *the old Adam*, sometimes *the flesh*, sometimes *his lower nature*, sometimes *his evil self*; and sometimes recognizes as simply that part of his being where God is not; then indeed is the man in the region of truth, and beginning to come true in himself. Nor will it be long ere he discover that there is no part in him with which he would be at strife, so God were there, so that it were true, what it ought to be—in right relation to the whole; for, by whatever name called, the old Adam, or antecedent horse, or dog, or tiger, it would then fulfil its part holily, intruding upon nothing, subject utterly to the rule of the higher; horse or dog or tiger, it would be good horse, good dog, good tiger.

When the man bows down before a power that can account for him, a power to whom he is no mystery as he is to himself; a power that knows whence he came and whither he is going; who knows why he loves this and hates that, why and where he began to go wrong; who can set him right, longs indeed to set him right, making of him a creature to look up to himself without shadow of doubt, anxiety or fear, confident as a child whom his father is leading by the hand to the heights of happy-making truth, knowing that where he is wrong, the father is right and will set him right; when the man feels his whole being in the embrace of self-responsible paternity—then the man is bursting into his flower; then the truth of his being, the eternal fact at the root of his new name, his real nature, his idea—born in God at first, and responsive to the truth, the being of God, his origin—begins to show itself; then his nature is almost in harmony with itself. For, obeying the will that is the cause of his being, the cause of that which demands of itself to be true, and that will being righteousness and love and truth, he begins to stand on the apex of his being, to know himself divine. He begins to feel himself free. The truth—not as known to his intellect, but as revealed in his own sense of being true, known by his essential consciousness of his divine condition, without which his nature is neither his own nor God's—trueness has made him free. Not any abstract truth, not all abstract truth, not truth its very metaphysical self, held by purest insight into entity, can make any man free; but the truth done, the truth loved, the truth lived by the man; the truth *of* and not merely *in* the man himself; the honesty that makes the man himself a child of the honest God.

When a man is, with his whole nature, loving and willing the truth, he is then a live truth. But this he has not originated in himself. He has seen it and striven for it, but not originated it. The one originating, living, visible truth, embracing all truths in all relations, is Jesus Christ. He is true; he is the live Truth. His truth, chosen and willed by him, the ripeness of his being, the flower of his sonship which is his nature, the crown of his one topmost perfect relation acknowledged and gloried in, is his absolute obedience to his father. The obedient Jesus is Jesus the Truth. He is true and the root of all truth and development of truth in men. Their very being, however far from the true human, is the undeveloped Christ in them, and his likeness to Christ is the truth of a man, even as the perfect meaning of a flower is the truth of a flower. Every man, according to the divine idea of him, must come to the truth of that idea; and under every form of Christ is the Christ. The truth of every man, I say, is the perfected Christ in him. As Christ is the blossom of humanity, so the blossom of every man is the Christ perfected in him. The vital force of humanity working in him is Christ; he is his root—the generator and perfecter of his individuality. The stronger the pure will of the man to be true; the freer and more active his choice; the more definite his individuality, ever the more is the man and all that is his, Christ's. Without him he could not have been; being, he could not have become capable of truth; capable of truth, he could never have loved it; loving and desiring it, he could not have attained to it. Nothing but the heart-presence, the humanest sympathy, and whatever deeper thing else may be betwixt the creating Truth and the responding soul, could make a man go on hoping, until at last he forget himself, and keep open house for God to come and go. He gives us the will wherewith to will, and the power to use it, and the help needed to supplement the power, whatever in any case the need may be; but we ourselves must will the truth, and for that the Lord is waiting, for the victory of God his father in the heart of his child. In this alone can he see of the travail of his soul, in this alone be satisfied. The work is his, but we must take our willing share. When the blossom breaks forth in us, the more it is ours the more it is his, for the highest creation of the Father, and that pre-eminently through the Son, is the being that can, like the Father and the Son, of his own self will what is right. The groaning and travailing, the blossom and the joy, are the Father's and the Son's and ours. The will, the power of willing, may be created, but the willing is begotten. Because God wills first, man wills also.

When my being is consciously and willedly in the hands of him who called it to live and think and suffer and be glad—given back to him by a perfect obedience—I thenceforward breathe the breath, share the life of God himself. Then I am free, in that I am true—which means one with the Father. And freedom knows itself to be freedom. When a man is true, if he were in hell he could not be miserable. He is right with himself because right with him whence he came. To be right with God is to be right with the universe; one with the power, the love, the will of the mighty Father, the cherisher of joy, the lord of laughter, whose are all glories, all hopes, who loves everything, and hates nothing but selfishness, which he will not have in his kingdom.

Christ then is the Lord of life; his life is the light of men; the light mirrored in them changes them into the image of him, the Truth; and thus *the Truth, who is the Son, makes them free.*

FREEDOM.

The Truth shall make you free. . . . Whosoever committeth sin, is the servant of sin. And the servant abideth not in the house for ever: but the Son abideth ever. If the Son therefore shall make you free, ye shall be free indeed.—*John* viii. 32, 34-36.

As this passage stands, I have not been able to make sense of it. No man could be in the house of the Father in virtue of being the servant of sin; yet this man is in the house as a servant, and the house in which he serves is not the house of sin, but the house of the Father. The utterance is confused at best, and the reasoning faulty. He must be in the house of the Father on some other ground than sin. This, had no help come, would have been sufficient cause for leaving the passage alone, as one where, perhaps, the words of the Lord were misrepresented—where, at least, perceiving more than one fundamental truth involved in the passage, I failed to follow the argument. I do not see that I could ever have suggested where the corruption, if any, lay. Most difficulties of similar nature have originated, like this, I can hardly doubt, with some scribe who, desiring to explain what he did not understand, wrote his worthless gloss on the margin: the next copier took the words for an omission that ought to be replaced in the body of the text, and inserting them, falsified the utterance, and greatly obscured its intention. What do we not owe to the critics who have searched the scriptures, and found what really was written! In the present case, Dr. Westcott's notation gives us to understand that there is another with 'a reasonable probability of being the true reading.' The difference is indeed small to the eye, but is great enough to give us fine gold instead of questionable ore. In an alternative of the kind, I must hope in what seems logical against what seems illogical; in what seems radiant against what seems trite.

What I take for the true reading then, I English thus: 'Every one committing sin is a slave. But the slave does not remain in the house for ever; the son remaineth for ever. If then the son shall make you free, you shall in reality be free.' The authorized version gives, 'Whosoever committeth sin, is the servant *of sin*;' the revised version gives,

'Every one that committeth sin is the bondservant *of sin*;' both accepting the reading that has the words, '*of sin.*' The statement is certainly in itself true, but appears to me useless for the argument that follows. And I think it may have been what I take to be the true reading, that suggested to the apostle Paul what he says in the beginning of the fourth chapter of his Epistle to the Galatians—words of spirit and life from which has been mistakenly drawn the doctrine of adoption, merest poison to the child-heart. The words of the Lord here are not that he who sins is the slave of sin, true utterly as that is; but that he is a slave, and the argument shows that he means a slave to God. The two are perfectly consistent. No amount of slavery to sin can keep a man from being as much the slave of God as God chooses in his mercy to make him. It is his sin makes him a slave instead of a child. His slavery to sin is his ruin; his slavery to God is his only hope. God indeed does not love slavery; he hates it; he will have children, not slaves; but he may keep a slave in his house a long time in the hope of waking up the poor slavish nature to aspire to the sonship which belongs to him, which is his birthright. But the slave is not to be in the house for ever. The father is not bound to keep his son a slave because the foolish child prefers it.

Whoever will not do what God desires of him, is a slave whom God can compel to do it, however he may bear with him. He who, knowing this, or fearing punishment, obeys God, is still a slave, but a slave who comes within hearing of the voice of his master. There are, however, far higher than he, who yet are but slaves. Those to whom God is not all in all, are slaves. They may not commit great sins; they may be trying to do right; but so long as they *serve* God, as they call it, from duty, and do not know him as their father, the joy of their being, they are slaves—good slaves, but slaves. If they did not try to do their duty, they would be bad slaves. They are by no means so slavish as those that serve from fear, but they are slaves; and because they are but slaves, they can fulfil no righteousness, can do no duty perfectly, but must ever be trying after it wearily and in pain, knowing well that if they stop trying, they are lost. They are slaves indeed, for they would be glad to be adopted by one who is their own father! Where then are the sons? I know none, I answer, who are yet utterly and entirely sons or daughters.

There may be such—God knows; I have not known them; or, knowing them, have not been myself such as to be able to recognize them. But I do know some who are enough sons and daughters to be at war with the slave in them, who are not content to be slaves to their father. Nothing I have seen or known of sonship, comes near the glory of the thing; but there are thousands of sons and daughters, though their number be yet only a remnant, who are siding with the father of their spirits against themselves, against all that divides them from him from whom they have come, but out of whom they have never come, seeing that in him they live and move and have their being. Such are not slaves; they are true though not perfect children; they are fighting along with God against the evil separation; they are breaking at the middle wall of partition. Only the rings of their fetters are left, and they are struggling to take them off. They are children—with more or less of the dying slave in them; they know it is there, and what it is, and hate the slavery in them, and try to slay it. The real slave is he who does not seek to be a child; who does not desire to end his slavery; who looks upon the claim of the child as presumption; who cleaves to the traditional authorized service of forms and ceremonies, and does not know the will of him who made the seven stars and Orion, much less cares to obey it; who never lifts up his heart to cry 'Father, what wouldst thou have me to do?' Such are continually betraying their slavery by their complaints. 'Do we not well to be angry?' they cry with Jonah; and, truly, being slaves, I do not know how they are to help it. When they are sons and daughters, they will no longer complain of the hardships, and miseries, and troubles of life; no longer grumble at their aches and pains, at the pinching of their poverty, at the hunger that assails them; no longer be indignant at their rejection by what is called Society. Those who believe in their own perfect father, can ill blame him for anything they do not like. Ah, friend, it may be you and I are slaves, but there *are* such sons and daughters as I speak of.

The slaves of sin rarely grumble at that slavery; it is their slavery to God they grumble at; of that alone they complain—of the painful messengers he sends to deliver them from their slavery both to sin and to himself. They must be sons or slaves. They cannot rid themselves of their owner. Whether they deny God, or mock him by acknowledging and not heeding him, or treat him as an arbitrary, formal monarch; whether, taking no trouble to find out what pleases him, they do dull things for his service he cares nothing about, or try to propitiate him by assuming with strenuous effort some yoke the Son never wore, and never called on them to wear, they are slaves, and not the less slaves that they are slaves to God; they are so thoroughly slaves, that they do not care to get out of their slavery by becoming sons and daughters, by finding the good of life where alone it can or could lie. Could a creator make a creature whose well-being should not depend on himself? And if he could, would the creature be the greater for that? Which, the creature he made more, or the creature he made less dependent on himself, would be the greater? The slave in heart would immediately, with Milton's Satan, reply, that the farthest from him who made him must be the freest, thus acknowledging his very existence a slavery, and but two kinds in being—a creator, and as many slaves as he pleases to make, whose refusal to obey is their unknown protest against their own essence. *Being* itself must, for what they call liberty, be repudiated! Creation itself, to go by their lines of life, is an injustice! God had no right to create beings less than himself; and as he could not create equal, he ought not to have created! But they do not complain of having been created; they complain of being required to do justice. They will not obey, but, his own handiwork, ravish from his work every advantage they can! They desire to be free with another kind of freedom than that with which God is free; unknowing, they seek a more complete slavery. There is, in truth, no mid way between absolute harmony with the Father and the condition of slaves—submissive, or rebellious. If the latter, their very rebellion is by the strength of the Father in them. Of divine essence, they thrust their existence in the face of their essence, their own nature.

Yet is their very rebellion in some sense but the rising in them of his spirit against their false notion of him—against the lies they hold concerning him. They do not see that, if his work, namely, they themselves, are the chief joy to themselves, much more might the life that works them be a glory and joy to them the work—inasmuch as it is nearer to them than they to themselves, causing them to be, and extends, without breach of relation, so infinitely above and beyond them. For nothing can come so close as that which creates; the nearest, strongest, dearest relation possible is between creator and created. Where this is denied, the schism is the widest; where it is acknowledged and fulfilled, the closeness is unspeakable. But ever remains what cannot be said, and I sink defeated. The very protest of the rebel against slavery, comes at once of the truth of God in him, which he cannot all cast from him, and of a slavery too low to love truth—a meanness that will take all and acknowledge nothing, as if his very being was a disgrace to him. The liberty of the God that would have his creature free, is in contest with the slavery of the creature who would cut his own stem from his root that he might call it his own and love it; who rejoices in his own consciousness, instead of the life of that consciousness; who poises himself on the tottering wall of his own being, instead of the rock on which that being is built. Such a one regards his own dominion over himself—the rule of the greater by the less, inasmuch as the conscious self is less than the self—

as a freedom infinitely greater than the range of the universe of God's being. If he says, 'At least I have it my own way!' I answer, You do not know what is your way and what is not. You know nothing of whence your impulses, your desires, your tendencies, your likings come. They may spring now from some chance, as of nerves diseased; now from some roar of a wandering bodiless devil; now from some infant hate in your heart; now from the greed or lawlessness of some ancestor you would be ashamed of if you knew him; or it may be now from some far-piercing chord of a heavenly orchestra: the moment it comes up into your consciousness, you call it your own way, and glory in it! Two devils amusing themselves with a duet of inspiration, one at each ear, might soon make that lordly *me* you are so in love with, rejoice in the freedom of willing the opposite each alternate moment; and at length drive you mad at finding that you could not, will as you would, make choice of a way and its opposite simultaneously. The whole question rests and turns on the relation of creative and created, of which relation few seem to have the consciousness yet developed. To live without the eternal creative life is an impossibility; freedom from God can only mean an incapacity for seeing the facts of existence, an incapability of understanding the glory of the creature who makes common cause with his creator in his creation of him, who wills that the lovely will calling him into life and giving him choice, should finish making him, should draw him into the circle of the creative heart, to joy that he lives by no poor power of his own will, but is one with the causing life of his life, in closest breathing and willing, vital and claimant oneness with the life of all life. Such a creature knows the life of the infinite Father as the very flame of his life, and joys that nothing is done or will be done in the universe in which the Father will not make him all of a sharer that it is possible for perfect generosity to make him. If you say this is irreverent, I doubt if you have seen the God manifest in Jesus. But all will be well, for the little god of your poor content will starve your soul to misery, and the terror of the eternal death creeping upon you, will compel you to seek a perfect father. Oh, ye hide-bound Christians, the Lord is not straitened, but ye are straitened in your narrow unwilling souls! Some of you need to be shamed before yourselves; some of you need the fire.

But one who reads may call out, in the agony and thirst of a child waking from a dream of endless seeking and no finding, 'I am bound like Lazarus in his grave-clothes! what am I to do?' Here is the answer, drawn from this parable of our Lord; for the saying is much like a parable, teaching more than it utters, appealing to the conscience and heart, not to the understanding: You are a slave; the slave has no hold on the house; only the sons and daughters have an abiding rest in the home of their father. God cannot have slaves about him always. You must give up your slavery, and be set free from it. That is what I am here for. If I make you free, you shall be free indeed; for I can make you free only by making you what you were meant to be, sons like myself. That is how alone the Son can work. But it is you who must become sons; you must will it, and I am here to help you.' It is as if he said, 'You shall have the freedom of my father's universe; for, free from yourselves, you will be free of his heart. Yourselves are your slavery. That is the darkness which you have loved rather than the light. You have given honour to yourselves, and not to the Father; you have sought honour from men, and not from the Father! Therefore, even in the house of your father, you have been but sojourning slaves. We in his family are all one; we have no party-spirit; we have no self-seeking: fall in with us, and you shall be free as we are free.'

If then the poor starved child cry—'How, Lord?' the answer will depend on what he means by that *how*. If he means, 'What plan wilt thou adopt? What is thy scheme for cutting my bonds and setting me free?' the answer may be a deepening of the darkness, a tightening of the bonds. But if he means, 'Lord, what wouldst thou have me to do?' the answer will not tarry. 'Give yourself to me to do what I tell you, to understand what I say, to be my good, obedient little brother, and I will wake in you the heart that my father put in you, the same kind of heart that I have, and it will grow to love the Father, altogether and absolutely, as mine does, till you are ready to be torn to pieces for him. Then you will know that you are at the heart of the universe, at the heart of every secret—at the heart of the

Father. Not till then will you be free, then free indeed!'

Christ died to save us, not from suffering, but from ourselves; not from injustice, far less from justice, but from being unjust. He died that we might live—but live as he lives, by dying as he died who died to himself that he might live unto God. If we do not die to ourselves, we cannot live to God, and he that does not live to God, is dead. 'Ye shall know the truth,' the Lord says, 'and the truth shall make you free. I am the truth, and you shall be free as I am free. To be free, you must be sons like me. To be free you must *be* that which you have to be, that which you are created. To be free you must give the answer of sons to the Father who calls you. To be free you must fear nothing but evil, care for nothing but the will of the Father, hold to him in absolute confidence and infinite expectation. He alone is to be trusted.' He has shown us the Father not only by doing what the Father does, not only by loving his Father's children even as the Father loves them, but by his perfect satisfaction with him, his joy in him, his utter obedience to him. He has shown us the Father by the absolute devotion of a perfect son. He is the Son of God because the Father and he are one, have one thought, one mind, one heart. Upon this truth —I do not mean the dogma, but the truth itself of Jesus to his father—hangs the universe ; and upon the recognition of this truth—that is, upon their becoming thus true—hangs the freedom of the children, the redemption of their whole world. 'I and the Father are one,' is the centre-truth of the universe ; and the circumfering truth is, 'that they also may be one in us.'

The only free man, then, is he who is a child of the Father. He is a servant of all, but can be made the slave of none : he is a son of the lord of the universe. He is in himself, in virtue of his truth, free. He is in himself a king. For the Son rests his claim to royalty on this, that *he was born and came into the world to bear witness to the truth.*

KINGSHIP.

Art thou a king then? Jesus answered, Thou sayest that I am a king! To this end was I born, and for this cause came I into the world, that I should bear witness unto the truth: every one that is of the truth heareth my voice.—John xviii. 37.

PILATE asks Jesus if he is a king. The question is called forth by what the Lord had just said concerning his kingdom, closing with the statement that it was not of this world. He now answers Pilate that he is a king indeed, but shows him that his kingdom is of a very different kind from what is called kingdom in this world. The rank and rule of this world are uninteresting to him. He might have had them. Calling his disciples to follow him, and his twelve legions of angels to help them, he might soon have driven the Romans into the abyss, piling them on the heap of nations they had tumbled there before. What easier for him than thus to have cleared the way, and over the tributary world reigned the just monarch that was the dream of the Jews, never seen in Israel or elsewhere, but haunting the hopes and longings of the poor and their helpers! He might from Jerusalem have ruled the world, not merely dispensing what men call justice, but compelling atonement. He did not care for government. No such kingdom would serve the ends of his father in heaven, or comfort his own soul. What was perfect empire to the Son of God, while he might teach one human being to love his neighbour, and be good like his father! To be love-helper to one heart, for its joy, and the glory of his father, was the beginning of true kingship! The Lord would rather wash the feet of his weary brothers, than be the one only perfect monarch that ever ruled in the world. It was empire he rejected when he ordered Satan behind him like a dog to his heel. Government, I repeat, was to him flat, stale, unprofitable.

What then is the kingdom over which the Lord cares to reign, for he says he came into the world to be a king? I answer, A kingdom of kings, and no other. Where every man is a king, there and there only does the Lord care to reign, in the name of his father. As no king in Europe would care to reign over a cannibal, a savage, or an animal race, so the Lord cares for no kingdom over anything this world calls a nation. A king must rule over his own kind. Jesus is a king in virtue of no conquest, inheritance, or election, but in right of essential being; and he cares for no subjects but such as are his subjects in the same right. His subjects must be of his own kind, in their very nature and essence kings. To understand his answer to Pilate, see wherein consists his kingship; what it is that makes him a king; what manifestation of his essential being gives him a claim to be king. The Lord's is a kingdom in which no man seeks to be above another: ambition is of the dirt of this world's kingdoms. He says, 'I am a king, for I was born for the purpose, I came into the world with the object of bearing witness to the truth. Everyone that is of my kind, that is of the truth, hears my voice. He is a king like me, and makes one of my subjects.' Pilate thereupon—as would most Christians nowadays, instead of setting about being true—requests a definition of truth, a presentation to his intellect in set terms of what the word 'truth' means; but instantly, whether confident of the uselessness of the inquiry, or intending to resume it when he has set the Lord at liberty, goes out to the people to tell them he finds no fault in him. Whatever interpretation we put on his action here, he must be far less worthy of blame than those 'Christians' who, instead of setting themselves to be pure 'even as he is pure,' to be their brother and sister's keeper, and to serve God by being honourable in shop and counting-house and labour-market, proceed to 'serve' him, some by going to church or chapel, some by condemning the opinions of their neighbours, some by teaching others what they do not themselves heed. Neither Pilate nor they ask the one true question, 'How am I to be a true man? How am I to become a man worth being a man?' The Lord is a king because his life, the life of his thoughts, of his imagination, of his will, of every smallest action, is true—true first to God in that he is altogether his, true to himself in that he forgets himself altogether, and true to his fellows in that he will endure anything they do to him, nor cease declaring himself the son and messenger and likeness of God. They will kill him, but it matters not: the truth is as he says!

Jesus is a king because his business is to bear witness to the truth. What truth? All truth; all verity of relation throughout the universe—first of all, that his father is good, perfectly good; and that the crown and joy of life is to desire and do the will of the eternal source of will, and of all life. He deals thus the death-blow to the power of hell. For the one principle of hell is—'I am my own. I am my own king and my own subject. *I* am the centre from which go out my thoughts; *I* am the object and end of my thoughts; back upon *me* as the alpha and omega of life, my thoughts return. My own glory is, and ought to be, my chief care; my ambition, to gather the regards of men to the one centre, myself. My pleasure is *my* pleasure. My kingdom is—as many as I can bring to acknowledge my greatness over them. My judgment is the faultless rule of things. My right is—what I desire. The more I am all in all to myself, the greater I am. The less I acknowledge debt or obligation to another; the more I close my eyes to the fact that I did not make myself; the more self-sufficing I feel or imagine myself—the greater I am. I will be free with the freedom that consists in doing whatever I am inclined to do, from whatever quarter may come the inclination. To do my own will so long as I feel anything to be my will, is to be free, is to live' To all these principles of hell, or of this world—they are the same thing, and it matters nothing whether they are asserted or defended so long as they are acted upon—the Lord, the king, gives the direct lie. It is as if he said:—' I ought to know what I say, for I have been from all eternity the son of him from whom you issue, and whom you call your father, but whom you will not have your father: I know all he thinks and is; and I say this, that my perfect freedom, my pure individuality, rests on the fact that I have not another will than his. My will is all for his will, for his will is right. He is righteousness itself. His very being is love and equity and self-devotion, and he will have his children such as himself—creatures of love, of fairness, of self-devotion to him and their fellows. I was born to bear witness to the truth—in my own person to be the truth visible—the very likeness and manifestation of the God who is true. My very being is his witness. Every fact of me witnesses him. He is the truth, and I am the truth. Kill me, but while I live I say, Such as I am he is. If I said I did not know him, I should be a liar. I fear nothing you can do to me. Shall the king who comes to say what is true, turn his back for fear of men? My Father is like me; I know it, and I say it. You do not like to hear it because you are not like him. I am low in your eyes which measure things by their show; therefore you say I blaspheme. I should blaspheme if I said he was such as anything you are capable of imagining him, for you love show, and power, and the praise of men. I do not, and God is like me. I came into the world to show him. I am a king because he sent me to bear witness to his truth, and I bear it. Kill me, and I will rise again. You can kill me, but you cannot hold me dead. Death is my servant; you are the slaves of Death because you will not be true, and let the truth make you free. Bound, and in your hands, I am free as God, for God is my father. I know I shall suffer, suffer unto death, but if you knew my father, you would not wonder that I am ready; you would be ready too. He is my strength. My father is greater than I.'

Remember, friends, I said, ' It is as if he said.' I am daring to present a shadow of the Lord's witnessing, a shadow surely cast by his deeds and his very words! If I mistake, he will forgive me. I do not fear him; I fear only lest, able to see and write these things, I should fail of witnessing, and myself be, after all, a castaway—no king, but a talker; no disciple of Jesus, ready to go with him to the death, but an arguer about the truth; a hater of the lies men speak for God, and myself a truth-speaking liar, not a doer of the word.

We see, then, that the Lord bore his witness to the Truth, to the one God, by standing just what he was, before the eyes and the lies of men. The true king is the man who stands up a true man and speaks the truth, and will die but not lie. The robes of such a king may be rags or purple; it matters neither way. The rags are the more likely, but neither better nor worse than the robes. Then was the Lord dressed most royally when his robes were a jest, a mockery, a laughter. Of the men who before Christ bare witness to the truth, some were sawn asunder, some subdued kingdoms; it mattered nothing which: they witnessed.

The truth is *God*; the witness to the truth is Jesus. The kingdom of the truth is the hearts of men. The bliss of men is the true God. The thought of God is the truth of everything. All well-being lies in true relation to God. The man who responds to this with his whole being, is of the truth. The man who knows these things, and but knows them; the man who sees them to be true, and does not order life and action, judgment and love by them, is of the worst of lying; with hand, and foot, and face he casts scorn upon that which his tongue confesses.

Little thought the sons of Zebedee and their ambitious mother what the earthly throne of Christ's glory was which they and she begged they might share. For the king crowned by his witnessing, witnessed then to the height of his uttermost argument, when he hung upon the cross—like a sin, as Paul in his boldness expresses it. When his witness is treated as a lie, then most he witnesses, for he gives it still. High and lifted up on the throne of his witness, on the cross of his torture, he holds to it: 'I and the Father are one.' Every mockery borne in witnessing, is a witnessing afresh. Infinitely more than had he sat on the throne of the whole earth, did Jesus witness to the truth when Pilate brought him out for the last time, and perhaps made him sit on the judgment-seat in his mockery of kingly garments and royal insignia, saying, 'Behold your king!' Just because of those robes

Kingship

and that crown, that sceptre and that throne of ridicule, he was the only real king that ever sat on any throne.

Is every Christian expected to bear witness? A man content to bear no witness to the truth is not in the kingdom of heaven. One who believes must bear witness. One who sees the truth, must live witnessing to it. Is our life, then, a witnessing to the truth? Do we carry ourselves in bank, on farm, in house or shop, in study or chamber or workshop, as the Lord would, or as the Lord would not? Are we careful to be true? Do we endeavour to live to the height of our ideas? Or are we mean, self-serving, world-flattering, fawning slaves? When contempt is cast on the truth, do we smile? Wronged in our presence, do we make no sign that we hold by it? I do not say we are called upon to dispute, and defend with logic and argument, but we are called upon to show that we are on the other side. But when I say *truth*, I do not mean *opinion*: to treat opinion as if that were truth, is grievously to wrong the truth. The soul that loves the truth and tries to be true, will know when to speak and when to be silent; but the true man will never look as if he did not care. We are not bound to say all we think, but we are bound not even to look what we do not think. The girl who said before a company of mocking companions, 'I believe in Jesus,' bore true witness to her Master, the Truth. David bore witness to God, the Truth, when he said, '*Unto thee, O Lord, belongeth mercy, for thou renderest to every man according to his work.*'

JUSTICE.

Also unto thee, O Lord, belongeth mercy; for thou renderest to every man according to his work.—*Psalm* lxii. 12.

SOME of the translators make it *kindness* and *goodness*; but I presume there is no real difference among them as to the character of the word which here, in the English Bible, is translated *mercy*.

The religious mind, however, educated upon the theories yet prevailing in the so-called religious world, must here recognize a departure from the presentation to which they have been accustomed: to make the psalm speak according to prevalent theoretic modes, the verse would have to be changed thus:—'To thee, O Lord, belongeth *justice*, for thou renderest to every man according to his work.'

Let the reason of my choosing this passage, so remarkable in itself, for a motto to the sermon which follows, remain for the present doubtful. I need hardly say that I mean to found no logical argument upon it.

Let us endeavour to see plainly what we mean when we use the word *justice*, and whether we mean what we ought to mean when we use it—especially with reference to God. Let us come nearer to knowing what we ought to understand by justice, that is, the justice of God; for his justice is the live, active justice, giving existence to the idea of justice in our minds and hearts. Because he is just, we are capable of knowing justice; it is because he is just, that we have the idea of justice so deeply imbedded in us.

What do we oftenest mean by *justice*? Is it not the carrying out of the law, the infliction of penalty assigned to offence? By a just judge we mean a man who administers the law without prejudice, without favour or dislike; and where guilt is manifest, punishes as much as, and no more than, the law has in the case laid down. It may not be that justice has therefore been done. The law itself may be unjust, and the judge may mistake; or, which is more likely, the working of the law may be foiled by the parasites of law for their own gain. But even if the law be good, and thoroughly administered, it does not necessarily follow that justice is done.

Suppose my watch has been taken from my pocket; I lay hold of the thief; he is dragged before the magistrate, proved guilty, and sentenced to a just imprisonment: must I walk home satisfied with the result? Have I had justice done me? The thief may have had justice done him—but where is my watch? That is gone, and I remain a man wronged. Who has done me the wrong? The thief. Who can set right the wrong? The thief, and only the thief; nobody but the man that did the wrong. God may be able to move the man to right the wrong, but God himself cannot right it without the man. Suppose my watch found and restored, is the account settled between me and the thief? I may forgive him, but is the wrong removed? By no means. But suppose the thief to bethink himself, to repent. He has, we shall say, put it out of his power to return the watch, but he comes to me and says he is sorry he stole it, and begs me to accept for the present what little he is able to bring, as a beginning of atonement: how should I then regard the matter? Should I not feel that he had gone far to make atonement—done more to make up for the injury he had inflicted upon me, than the mere restoration of the watch, even by himself, could reach to? Would there not lie, in the thief's confession and submission and initial restoration, an appeal to the divinest in me—to the eternal brotherhood? Would it not indeed amount to a sufficing atonement as between man and man? If he offered to bear what I chose to lay upon him, should I feel it necessary, for the sake of justice, to inflict some certain suffering as demanded by righteousness? I should still have a claim upon him for my watch, but should I not be apt to forget it? He who commits the offence can make up for it—and he alone.

One thing must surely be plain—that the punishment of the wrong-doer makes no atonement for the wrong done. How could it make up to me for the stealing of my watch that the man was punished? The wrong would be there all the same. I am not saying the man ought not to be punished—far from it; I am only saying that the punishment nowise makes up to the man wronged. Suppose the man, with the watch in his pocket, were to inflict the severest flagellation on himself: would that lessen my sense of injury? Would it set anything right? Would it anyway atone? Would it give him a right to the watch? Punishment may do good to the man who does the wrong, but that is a thing as different as important.

Another thing plain is, that, even without the material rectification of the wrong where that is impossible, repentance removes the offence which no suffering could. I at least should feel that I had no more quarrel with the man. I should even feel that the gift he had made me, giving into my heart a repentant brother, was infinitely beyond the restitution of what he had taken from me. True, he owed me both himself and the watch, but such a greater does more than include such a less. If it be objected, 'You may forgive, but the man has sinned against God!'—Then it is not a part of the divine to be merciful, I return, and a man may be more merciful than his maker! A man may do that which would be too merciful in God! Then mercy is not a divine attribute, for it may exceed and be too much; it must not be infinite, therefore cannot be God's own.

'Mercy may be against justice.' Never—if you mean by justice what I mean by justice. If anything be against justice, it cannot be called mercy, for it is cruelty. *'To thee, O Lord, belongeth mercy, for thou renderest to every man according to his work.'*

There is *no* opposition, *no* strife whatever, between mercy and justice. Those who say justice means the punishing of sin, and mercy the not punishing of sin, and attribute both to God, would make a schism in the very idea of God. And this brings me to the question, What is meant by divine justice?

Human justice may be a poor distortion of justice, a mere shadow of it; but the justice of God must be perfect. We cannot frustrate it in its working; are we just to it in our idea of it? If you ask any ordinary Sunday congregation in England, what is meant by the justice of God, would not nineteen out of twenty answer, that it means his punishing of sin? Think for a moment what degree of justice it would indicate in a man—that he punished every wrong. A Roman emperor, a Turkish cadi, might do that, and be the most unjust both of men and judges. Ahab might be just on the throne of punishment, and in his garden the murderer of Naboth. In God shall we imagine a distinction of office and character? God is one; and the depth of foolishness is reached by that theology which talks of God as if he held different offices, and differed in each. It sets a contradiction in the very nature of God himself. It represents him, for instance, as having to do that as a magistrate which as a father he would not do! The love of the father makes him desire to be unjust as a magistrate! Oh the folly of any mind that would explain God before obeying him! that would map out the character of God, instead of crying, Lord, what wouldst thou have me to do? God is no magistrate; but, if he were, it would be a position to which his fatherhood alone gave him the right; his rights as a father cover every right he can be analytically supposed to possess. The justice of God is this, that—to use a boyish phrase, the best the language will now afford me because of misuse—he gives every man, woman, child, and beast, everything that has being, *fair play*; he renders to every man according to his work; and therein lies his perfect mercy; for nothing else could be merciful to the man, and nothing but mercy could be fair to him. God does nothing of which any just man, the thing set fairly and fully before him so that he understood, would not say, 'That is fair.' Who would, I repeat, say a man was a just man because he insisted on prosecuting every offender? A scoundrel might do that. Yet the justice of God, forsooth, is his punishment of sin! A just man is one who cares, and tries, and always tries, to give fair play to everyone in everything. When we speak of the justice of God, let us see that we do mean justice! Punishment of the guilty may be involved in justice, but it does not constitute the justice of God one atom more than it would constitute the justice of a man.

'But no one ever doubts that God gives fair play!'

'That may be—but does not go for much, if you say that God does this or that which is not fair.'

'If he does it, you may be sure it is fair.'

'Doubtless, or he could not be God—except to devils. But you say he does so and so, and is just; I say, he does not do so and so, and is just. You say he does, for the Bible says so. I say, if the Bible said so, the Bible would lie; but the Bible does not say so. The lord of life complains of men for not judging right. To say on the authority of the Bible that God does a thing no honourable man would do, is to lie against God; to say that it is therefore right, is to lie against the very spirit of God. To uphold a lie for God's sake is to be against God, not for him. God cannot be lied for.

He is the truth. The truth alone is on his side. While his child could not see the rectitude of a thing, he would infinitely rather, even if the thing were right, have him say, God could not do that thing, than have him believe that he did it. If the man were sure God did it, the thing he ought to say would be, 'Then there must be something about it I do not know, which if I did know, I should see the thing quite differently.' But where an evil thing is invented to explain and account for a good thing, and a lover of God is called upon to believe the invention or be cast out, he needs not mind being cast out, for it is into the company of Jesus. Where there is no ground to believe that God does a thing except that men who would explain God have believed and taught it, he is not a true man who accepts men against his own conscience of God. I acknowledge no authority calling upon me to believe a thing of God, which I could not be a man and believe right in my fellow-man. I will accept no explanation of any way of God which explanation involves what I should scorn as false and unfair in a man. If you say, That may be right of God to do which it would not be right of man to do, I answer, Yes, because the relation of the maker to his creatures is very different from the relation of one of those creatures to another, and he has therefore duties toward his creatures requiring of him what no man would have the right to do to his fellow-man; but he can have no duty that is not both just and merciful. More is required of the maker, by his own act of creation, than can be required of men. More and higher justice and righteousness is required of him by himself, the Truth;—greater nobleness, more penetrating sympathy; and *nothing* but what, if an honest man understood it, he would say was right. If it be a thing man cannot understand, then man can say nothing as to whether it is right or wrong. He cannot even know that God does *it*, when the *it* is unintelligible to him. What he calls *it* may be but the smallest facet of a composite action. His part is silence. If it be said by any that God does a thing, and the thing seems to me unjust, then either I do not know what the thing is, or God does not do it. The saying cannot mean what it seems to mean, or the saying is not true. If, for instance, it be said that God visits the sins of the fathers on the children, a man who takes *visits upon* to mean *punishes*, and *the children* to mean *the innocent children*, ought to say, 'Either I do not understand the statement, or the thing is not true, whoever says it.' God *may* do what seems to a man not right, but it must so seem to him because God works on higher, on divine, on perfect principles, too right for a selfish, unfair, or unloving man to understand. But least of all must we accept some low notion of justice in a man, and argue that God is just in doing after that notion.

The common idea, then, is, that the justice of God consists in punishing sin: it is in the hope of giving a larger idea of the justice of God in punishing sin that I ask, '*Why is God bound to punish sin?*'

'How could he be a just God and not punish sin?'

'Mercy is a good and right thing,' I answer, 'and but for sin there could be no mercy. We are enjoined to forgive, to be merciful, to be as our father in heaven. Two rights cannot possibly be opposed to each other. If God punish sin, it must be merciful to punish sin; and if God forgive sin, it must be just to forgive sin. We are required to forgive, with the argument that our father forgives. It must, I say, be right to forgive. Every attribute of God must be infinite as himself. He cannot be sometimes merciful, and not always merciful. He cannot be just, and not always just. Mercy belongs to him, and needs no contrivance of theologic chicanery to justify it.'

'Then you mean that it is wrong to punish sin, therefore God does not punish sin?'

'By no means; God does punish sin, but there is no opposition between punishment and forgiveness. The one may be essential to the possibility of the other. *Why*, I repeat, does God punish sin? That is my point.'

'Because in itself sin deserves punishment.'

'Then how can he tell us to forgive it?'

'He punishes, and having punished he forgives?'

'That will hardly do. If sin demands punishment, and the righteous punishment is given, then the man is free. Why should he be forgiven?'

'He needs forgiveness because no amount of punishment will meet his deserts.'

I avoid for the present, as anyone may perceive, the probable expansion of this reply.

'Then why not forgive him at once if the punishment is not essential—if part can be pretermitted? And again, can that be required which, according to your showing, is not adequate? You will perhaps answer, 'God may please to take what little he can have;' and this brings me to the fault in the whole idea.

Punishment is *nowise* an *offset* to sin. Foolish people sometimes, in a tone of self-gratulatory pity, will say, ' If I have sinned I have suffered.' Yes, verily, but what of that? What merit is there in it? Even had you laid the suffering upon yourself, what did that do to make up for the wrong? That you may have bettered by your suffering is well for you, but what atonement is there in the suffering? The notion is a false one altogether. Punishment, deserved suffering, is no equipoise to sin. It is no use laying it in the other scale. It will not move it a hair's breadth. Suffering weighs nothing at all against sin. It is not of the same kind, not under the same laws, any more than mind and matter. We say a man deserves punishment; but when we forgive and do not punish him, we do not *always* feel that we have done wrong; neither when we do punish him do we feel that any amends has been made for his wrongdoing. If it were an offset to wrong, then God would be bound to punish for the sake of the punishment; but he cannot be, for he forgives. Then it is not for the sake of the punishment, as a thing that in itself ought to be done, but for the sake of something else, as a means to an end, that God punishes. It is not directly for justice, else how could he show mercy, for that would involve injustice?

Primarily, God is not bound to *punish* sin; he is bound to *destroy* sin. If he were not the Maker, he might not be bound to destroy sin—I do not know; but seeing he has created creatures who have sinned, and therefore sin has, by the creating act of God, come into the world, God is, in his own righteousness, bound to destroy sin.

'But that is to have no mercy.'

You mistake. God does destroy sin; he is always destroying sin. In him I trust that he is destroying sin in me. He is always saving the sinner from his sins, and that is destroying sin. But vengeance on the sinner, the law of a tooth for a tooth, is not in the heart of God, neither in his hand. If the sinner and the sin in him, are the concrete object of the divine wrath, then indeed there can be no mercy. Then indeed there will be an end put to sin by the destruction of the sin and the sinner together. But thus would no atonement be wrought—nothing be done to make up for the wrong God has allowed to come into being by creating man. There must be an atonement, a making-up, a bringing together—an atonement which, I say, cannot be made except by the man who has sinned.

Punishment, I repeat, is not the thing required of God, but the absolute destruction of sin. What better is the world, what better is the sinner, what better is God, what better is the truth, that the sinner should suffer—continue suffering to all eternity? Would there be less sin in the universe? Would there be any making-up for sin? Would it show God justified in doing what he knew would bring sin into the world, justified in making creatures who he knew would sin? What setting-right would come of the sinner's suffering? If justice demand it, if suffering be the equivalent for sin, then the sinner must suffer, then God is bound to exact his suffering, and not pardon; and so the making of man was a tyrannical deed, a creative cruelty. But grant that the sinner has deserved to suffer, no amount of suffering is any atonement for his sin. To suffer to all eternity could not make up for one unjust word. Does that mean, then, that for an unjust word I deserve to suffer to all eternity? The unjust word is an eternally evil thing; nothing but God in my heart can cleanse me from the evil that uttered it; but does it follow that I saw the evil of what I did so perfectly, that eternal punishment for it would be just? Sorrow and confession and self-abasing love will make up for the evil word; suffering will not. For evil in the abstract, nothing can be done. It is eternally evil. But I may be saved from it by learning to loathe it, to hate it, to shrink from it with an eternal avoidance. The only vengeance worth having on sin is to make the sinner himself its executioner. Sin and punishment are in no antagonism to each other in man, any more than pardon and punishment are in God; they can perfectly co-exist. The one naturally follows the other, punishment being born of sin, because evil exists only by the life of good, and has no life of its own, being in itself death. Sin and suffering are not natural opposites; the opposite of evil is good, not suffering; the opposite of sin is not suffering, but righteousness. The path across the gulf that divides right from wrong is not the fire, but repentance. If my friend has wronged me, will it console me to see him punished? Will that be a rendering to me of my due? Will his agony be a balm to my deep wound? Should I be fit for any friendship if that were possible even in regard to my enemy? But would not the shadow of repentant grief, the light of reviving love on his countenance, heal it at once however deep? Take any of those wicked people in Dante's hell, and ask wherein is justice served by their punishment. Mind, I am not saying it is not right to punish them; I am saying that justice is not, never can be, satisfied by suffering—nay, cannot have any satisfaction in or from suffering. Human resentment, human revenge, human hate may. Such justice as Dante's keeps wickedness alive in its most terrible forms. The life of God goes forth to inform, or at least give a home to victorious evil. Is he not defeated every time that one of those lost souls defies him? All hell cannot make Vanni Fucci say 'I was wrong.' God is triumphantly defeated, I say, throughout the hell of his vengeance. Although against evil, it is but the vain and wasted cruelty of a tyrant. There is no destruction of evil thereby, but an enhancing of its horrible power in the midst of the most agonizing and disgusting tortures a *divine* imagination can invent. If sin must be kept alive, then hell must be kept alive; but while I regard the smallest sin as infinitely loathsome, I do not believe that any being, never good enough to see the essential ugliness of sin, could sin so as to *deserve* such punishment. I am not now, however, dealing with the question of the duration of punishment, but with the idea of punishment itself; and would only say in passing, that the notion that a creature born imperfect, nay, born with impulses to evil not of his own generating, and which he could not help having, a creature to whom the true face of God was never presented, and by whom it never could have been seen, should be thus condemned, is as loathsome a lie against God as could find place in heart too undeveloped to understand what justice is, and too low to look up into the face of Jesus. It never in truth found place in any heart, though in many a pettifogging brain. There is but one thing lower than deliberately to believe such a lie, and that is to worship the God of whom it is believed. The one deepest, highest, truest, fittest, most wholesome suffering must be generated in the wicked by a vision, a true sight, more or less adequate, of the hideousness of their lives, of the horror of the wrongs they have done. Physical suffering may be a factor in rousing this mental pain; but 'I would I had never been born!' must be the cry of Judas, not because of the hell-fire around him, but because he loathes the man that betrayed his friend, the world's friend. When a man loathes himself, he has begun to be saved. Punishment tends to this result. Not for its own sake, not as a make-up for sin, not for divine revenge—horrible word, not for any satisfaction to justice, can punishment exist. Punishment is for the sake of amendment and atonement. God is bound by his love to punish sin in order to deliver his creature; he is bound by his justice to destroy sin in his creation. Love is justice—is the fulfilling of the law, for God as well as for his children. This is the reason of punishment; this is why justice requires that the wicked shall not go unpunished—that they, through the eye-opening power of pain, may come to see and do justice, may be brought to desire and make all possible amends, and so become just. Such punishment concerns justice in the deepest degree. For Justice, that is God, is bound in himself to see justice done by his children—not in the mere outward act, but in their very being. He is bound in himself to make up for wrong done by his children, and he can do nothing to make up for wrong done but by bringing about the repentance of the wrongdoer. When the man says, 'I did wrong; I hate myself and my deed; I cannot endure to think that I did it!' then, I say, is atonement begun. Without that, all that the Lord did would be lost. He would have made no atonement. Repentance, restitution, confession, prayer for forgiveness, righteous dealing thereafter, is the sole possible, the only true make-up for sin. For nothing less than this did Christ die. When a man acknowledges the right he denied before; when he says to the wrong, 'I abjure, I loathe you; I see now what you are; I could not see it before because I would not; God forgive me; make me clean, or let me die!' then justice, that is God, has conquered—and not till then.

'What atonement is there?'

Every atonement that God cares for; and the work of Jesus Christ on earth was the creative atonement, because it works atonement in every heart. He brings and is bringing God and man, and man and man, into perfect unity: 'I in them and thou in me, that they may be made perfect in one.'

'That is a dangerous doctrine!'

More dangerous than you think to many things—to every evil, to every lie, and among the rest to every false trust in what Christ did, instead of in Christ himself. Paul glories in the cross of Christ, but he does not trust in the cross: he trusts in the living Christ and his living father.

Justice then requires that sin should be put an end to; and not that only, but that it should be atoned for; and where punishment can do anything to this end, where it can help the sinner to know what he has been guilty of, where it can soften his heart to see his pride and wrong and cruelty, justice requires that punishment shall not be spared. And the more we believe in God, the surer we shall be that he will spare nothing that suffering can do to deliver his child from death. If suffering cannot serve this end, we need look for no more hell, but for the destruction of sin by the destruction of the sinner. That, however, would, it appears to me, be for God to suffer defeat, blameless indeed, but defeat.

If God be defeated, he must destroy—that is, he must withdraw life. How can he go on sending forth his life into irreclaimable souls, to keep sin alive in them throughout the ages of eternity? But then, I say, no atonement would be made for the wrongs they have done; God remains defeated, for he has created that which sinned, and which would not repent and make up for its sin. But those who believe that God will thus be defeated by many souls, must surely be of those who do not believe he cares enough to do his very best for them. He *is* their Father; he had power to make them out of himself, separate from himself, and capable of being one with him: surely he will somehow save and keep them! Not the power of sin itself can close *all* the channels between creating and created.

The notion of suffering as an offset for sin, the foolish idea that a man by suffering borne may get out from under the hostile claim to which his wrong-doing has subjected him, comes first of all, I think, from the satisfaction we feel when wrong comes to grief. Why do we feel this satisfaction? Because we hate wrong, but, not being righteous ourselves, more or less hate the wronger as well as his wrong, hence are not only righteously pleased to behold the law's disapproval proclaimed in his punishment, but unrighteously pleased with his suffering, because of the impact upon us of his wrong. In this way the inborn justice of our nature passes over to evil. It is no pleasure to God, as it so often is to us, to see the wicked suffer. To regard any suffering with satisfaction, save it be sympathetically with its curative quality, comes of evil, is inhuman because undivine, is a thing God is incapable of. His nature is always to forgive, and just because he forgives, he punishes. Because God is so altogether alien to wrong, because it is to him a heart-pain and trouble that one of his little ones should do the evil thing, there is, I believe, no extreme of suffering to which, for the sake of destroying the evil thing in them, he would not subject them. A man might flatter, or bribe, or coax a tyrant ; but there is no refuge from the love of God ; that love will, for very love, insist upon the uttermost farthing.

'That is not the sort of love I care about!'

No; how should you? I well believe it! You cannot care for it until you begin to know it. But the eternal love will not be moved to yield you to the selfishness that is killing you. What lover would yield his lady to her passion for morphia? You may sneer at such love, but the Son of God who took the weight of that love, and bore it through the world, is content with it, and so is everyone who knows it. The love of the Father is a radiant perfection. Love and not self-love is lord of the universe. Justice demands your punishment, because justice demands, and will have, the destruction of sin. Justice demands your punishment because it demands that your father should do his best for you. God, being the God of justice, that is of fair-play, and having made us what we are, apt to fall and capable of being raised again, is in himself bound to punish in order to deliver us—else is his relation to us poor beside that of an earthly father. 'To thee, O Lord, belongeth mercy, for thou renderest to every man according to his work.' A man's work is his character; and God in his mercy is not indifferent, but treats him according to his work.

The notion that the salvation of Jesus is a salvation from the consequences of our sins, is a false, mean, low notion. The salvation of Christ is salvation from the smallest tendency or leaning to sin.

It is a deliverance into the pure air of God's ways of thinking and feeling. It is a salvation that makes the heart pure, with the will and choice of the heart to be pure. To such a heart, sin is disgusting. It sees a thing as it is,—that is, as God sees it, for God sees everything as it is. The soul thus saved would rather sink into the flames of hell than steal into heaven and skulk there under the shadow of an imputed righteousness. No soul is saved that would not prefer hell to sin. Jesus did not die to save us from punishment; he was called Jesus because he should save his people from their sins.

If punishment be no atonement, how does the fact bear on the popular theology accepted by every one of the opposers of what they call Christianity, as representing its doctrines? Most of us have been more or less trained in it, and not a few of us have thereby, thank God, learned what it is —an evil thing, to be cast out of intellect and heart. Many imagine it dead and gone, but in reality it lies at the root (the intellectual root only, thank God) of much the greater part of the teaching of Christianity in the country; and is believed in—so far as the false *can* be believed in—by many who think they have left it behind, when they have merely omitted the truest, most offensive modes of expressing its doctrines. It is humiliating to find how many comparatively honest people think they get rid of a falsehood by softening the statement of it, by giving it the shape and placing it in the light in which it will least assert itself, and so have a good chance of passing both with such as hold it thoroughly, and such as might revolt against it more plainly uttered.

Once for all I will ease my soul regarding the horrid phantasm. I have passed through no change of opinion concerning it since first I began to write or speak; but I have written little and spoken less about it, because I would preach no mere negation. My work was not to destroy the false, except as it came in the way of building the true. Therefore I sought to speak but what I believed, saying little concerning what I did not believe; trusting, as now I trust, in the true to cast out the false, and shunning dispute. Neither will I now enter any theological lists to be the champion for or against mere doctrine. I have no desire to change the opinion of man or woman. Let everyone for me hold what he pleases. But I would do my utmost to disable such as think correct opinion essential to salvation from laying any other burden on the shoulders of true men and women than the yoke of their Master; and such burden, if already oppressing any, I would gladly lift. Let the Lord himself teach them, I say. A man who has not the mind of Christ—and no man has the mind of Christ except him who makes it his business to obey him—cannot have correct opinions concerning him; neither, if he could, would they be of any value to him: he would be nothing the better, he would be the worse for having them. Our business is not to think correctly, but to live truly; then first will there be a possibility of our thinking correctly. One chief cause of the amount of unbelief in the world is, that those who have seen something of the glory of Christ, set themselves to theorize concerning him rather than to obey him. In teaching men, they have not taught them Christ, but taught them about Christ. More eager after credible theory than after doing the truth, they have speculated in a condition of heart in which it was impossible they should understand; they have presumed to explain a Christ whom years and years of obedience could alone have made them able to comprehend. Their teaching of him, therefore, has been repugnant to the common sense of many who had not half their privileges, but in whom, as in Nathanael, there was no guile. Such, naturally, press their theories, in general derived from them of old time, upon others, insisting on their thinking about Christ as they think, instead of urging them to go to Christ to be taught by him whatever he chooses to teach them. They do their unintentional worst to stop all growth, all life. From such and their false teaching I would gladly help to deliver the true-hearted. Let the dead bury their dead, but I would do what I may to keep them from burying the living.

If there be no satisfaction to justice in the mere punishment of the wrong-doer, what shall we say of the notion of satisfying justice by causing one to suffer who is not the wrong-doer? And what, moreover, shall we say to the notion that, just because he is not the person who deserves to be punished, but is absolutely innocent, his suffering gives perfect satisfaction to the perfect justice? That the injustice be done with the consent of the person maltreated makes no difference: it makes it even worse, seeing, as they say, that justice requires the punishment of the *sinner*, and here is one far more than innocent. They have shifted their ground; it is no more punishment, but mere suffering the law requires! The thing gets worse and worse. I declare my utter and absolute repudiation of the idea in any form whatever. Rather than believe in a justice—that is, a God —to whose righteousness, abstract or concrete, it could be any satisfaction for the wrong-doing of a man that a man who did no wrong should suffer, I would be driven from among men, and dwell with the wild beasts that have not reason enough to be unreasonable. What! God, the father of Jesus Christ, like that! His justice contented with direst injustice! The anger of him who will nowise clear the guilty, appeased by the suffering of the innocent! Very God forbid! Observe: the evil fancy actually substitutes for punishment not mere suffering, but that suffering which is farthest from punishment; and this when, as I have shown, punishment, the severest, can be no satisfaction to justice! How did it come ever to be imagined? It sprang from the trustless dread that cannot believe in the forgiveness of the Father; cannot believe that even God will do anything for nothing; cannot trust him without a legal arrangement to bind him. How many, failing to trust God, fall back on *a text*, as they call it! It sprang from the pride that will understand what it cannot, before it will obey what it sees. He that will understand *first* will believe a lie—a lie from which obedience alone will at length deliver him. If anyone say, 'But I believe what you despise,' I answer, To believe it is your punishment for being able to believe it; you may call it your reward, if you will. You ought not to be able to believe it. It is the merest, poorest, most shameless fiction, invented without the perception that it was an invention—fit to satisfy the intellect, doubtless, of the inventor, else he could not have invented it. It has seemed to satisfy also many a humble soul, content to take what was given, and not think; content that another should think for him, and tell him what was the mind of his Father in heaven. Again I say, let the person who can be so satisfied be so satisfied; I have not to trouble myself with him. That he can be content with it, argues him unready to receive better. So long as he can believe false things concerning God, he is such as is capable of believing them—with how much or how little of blame, God knows. Opinion, right or wrong, will do nothing to save him. I would that he thought no more about this or any other opinion, but set himself to do the work of the Master. With his opinions, true or false, I have nothing to do. It is because such as he force evil things upon their fellows—utter or imply them from the seat of authority or influence—to their agony, their paralysation, their unbelief, their indignation, their stumbling, that I have any right to speak. I would save my fellows from having what notion of God is possible to them blotted out by a lie.

If it be asked how, if it be false, the doctrine of substitution can have been permitted to remain so long an article of faith to so many, I answer, On the same principle on which God took up and made use of the sacrifices men had, in their lack of faith, invented as a way of pleasing him. Some children will tell lies to please the parents that hate lying. They will even confess to having done a wrong they have not done, thinking their parents would like them to say they had done it, because they teach them to confess. God accepted men's sacrifices until he could get them to see—

and with how many has he yet not succeeded, in the church and out of it!—that he does not care for such things.

'But,' again it may well be asked, 'whence then has sprung the undeniable potency of that teaching?'

I answer, From its having in it a notion of God and his Christ, poor indeed and faint, but, by the very poverty and untruth in its presentation, fitted to the weakness and unbelief of men, seeing it was by men invented to meet and ease the demand made upon their own weakness and unbelief. Thus the leaven spreads. The truth is there. It is Christ the glory of God. But the ideas that poor slavish souls breed concerning this glory the moment the darkness begins to disperse, is quite another thing. Truth is indeed too good for men to believe; they must dilute it before they can take it; they must dilute it before they dare give it. They must make it less true before they can believe it enough to get any good of it. Unable to believe in the love of the Lord Jesus Christ, they invented a mediator in his mother, and so were able to approach a little where else they had stood away; unable to believe in the forgivingness of their father in heaven, they invented a way to be forgiven that should not demand of him so much; which might make it right for him to forgive; which should save them from having to believe downright in the tenderness of his father-heart, for that they found impossible. They thought him bound to punish for the sake of punishing, as an offset to their sin; they could not believe in clear forgiveness; that did not seem divine; it needed itself to be justified; so they invented for its justification a horrible injustice, involving all that was bad in sacrifice, even human sacrifice. They invented a satisfaction for sin which was an insult to God. He sought no satisfaction, but an obedient return to the Father. What satisfaction was needed he made himself in what he did to cause them to turn from evil and go back to him. The thing was too simple for complicated unbelief and the arguing spirit. Gladly would I help their followers to loathe such thoughts of God; but for that, they themselves must grow better men and women. While they are capable of being satisfied with them, there would be no advantage in their becoming intellectually convinced that such thoughts were wrong. I would not speak a word to persuade them of it.

Success would be worthless. They would but remain what they were—children capable of thinking meanly of their father. When the heart recoils, discovering how horrible it would be to have such an unreality for God, it will begin to search about and see whether it must indeed accept such statements concerning God; it will search after a real God by whom to hold fast, a real God to deliver them from the terrible idol. It is for those thus moved that I write, not at all for the sake of disputing with those who love the lie they may not be to blame for holding; who, like the Jews of old, would cast out of their synagogue the man who doubts the genuineness of their moral caricature of God, who doubts their travesty of the grandest truth in the universe, the atonement of Jesus Christ. Of such a man they will unhesitatingly report that he does not believe in the atonement. But a lie for God is against God, and carries the sentence of death in itself.

Instead of giving their energy to do the will of God, men of power have given it to the construction of a system by which to explain why Christ must die, what were the necessities and designs of God in permitting his death; and men of power of our own day, while casting from them not a little of the good in the teaching of the Roman Church, have clung to the morally and spiritually vulgar idea of justice and satisfaction held by pagan Rome, buttressed by the Jewish notion of sacrifice, and in its very home, alas, with the mother of all the western churches! Better the reformers had kept their belief in a purgatory, and parted with what is called vicarious sacrifice!

Their system is briefly this: God is bound to punish sin, and to punish it to the uttermost. His justice requires that sin be punished. But he loves man, and does not want to punish him if he can help it. Jesus Christ says, 'I will take his punishment upon me.' God accepts his offer, and lets man go unpunished—upon a condition. His justice is more than satisfied by the punishment of an infinite being instead of a world of worthless creatures. The suffering of Jesus is of greater value than that of all the generations, through endless ages, because he is infinite, pure, perfect in love and truth, being God's own everlasting son. God's condition with man is, that he believe in Christ's atonement thus explained. A man must say, 'I have sinned, and deserve to be tortured to all eternity. But Christ has paid my debts, by being punished instead of me. Therefore he is my Saviour. I am now bound by gratitude to him to turn away from evil.' Some would doubtless insist on his saying a good deal more, but this is enough for my purpose.

As to the justice of God requiring the punishment of the sinner, I have said enough. That the mere suffering of the sinner can be no satisfaction to justice, I have also tried to show. If the suffering of the sinner be indeed required by the justice of God, let it be administered. But what shall we say adequate to confront the base representation that it is not punishment, not the suffering of the sinner that is required, but suffering! nay, as if this were not depth enough of baseness to crown all heathenish representation of the ways of God, that the suffering of the innocent is unspeakably preferable in his eyes to that of the wicked, as a make-up for wrong done! nay, again, 'in the lowest deep a lower deep,' that the suffering of the holy, the suffering of the loving, the suffering of the eternally and perfectly good, is supremely satisfactory to the pure justice of the Father of spirits! Not all the suffering that could be heaped upon the wicked could buy them a moment's respite, so little is their suffering a counterpoise to their wrong; in the working of this law of equivalents, this *lex talionis*, the suffering of millions of years could not equal the sin of a moment, could not pay off one farthing of the deep debt. But so much more valuable, precious, and dear, is the suffering of the innocent, so much more of a satisfaction—observe—to the *justice* of God, that in return for that suffering another wrong is done: the sinners who deserve and ought to be punished are set free.

I know the root of all that can be said on the subject; the notion is imbedded in the gray matter of my Scotch brains; and if I reject it, I know what I reject. For the love of God my heart rose early against the low invention. Strange that in a Christian land it should need to be said, that to punish the innocent and let the guilty go free is unjust! It wrongs the innocent, the guilty, and God himself. It would be the worst of all wrongs to the guilty to treat them as innocent. The whole device is a piece of spiritual charlatanry—fit only for a fraudulent jail-delivery. If the wicked ought to be punished, it were the worst possible perversion of justice to take a righteous being however strong, and punish him instead of the sinner however weak. To the poorest idea of justice in punishment, it is essential that the sinner, and no other than the sinner, should receive the punishment. The strong being that was willing to bear such punishment might well be regarded as worshipful, but what of the God whose so-called justice he thus defeats? If you say it is justice, not God that demands the suffering, I say justice cannot demand that which is unjust, and the whole thing is unjust. God is absolutely just, and there is no deliverance from his justice, which is one with his mercy. The device is an absurdity—a grotesquely deformed absurdity. To represent the living God as a party to such a style of action, is to veil with a mask of cruelty and hypocrisy the face whose glory can be seen only in the face of Jesus; to put a tirade of vulgar Roman legality into the mouth of the Lord God merciful and gracious, who will by no means clear the guilty. Rather than believe such ugly folly of him whose very name is enough to make those that know him heave the breath of the hart panting for the waterbrooks; rather than think of him what in a man would make me avoid him at the risk of my life, I would say, 'There is no God; let us neither eat nor drink, that we may die! For lo, this is not our God! This is not he for whom we have waited!' But I have seen his face and heard his voice in the face and the voice of Jesus Christ; and I say this is our God, the very one whose being the Creator makes it an infinite gladness to be the created. I will not have the God of the scribes and the pharisees whether Jewish or Christian, protestant, Roman, or Greek, but thy father, O Christ! He is my God. If you say, 'That is our God, not yours!' I answer, 'Your portrait of your God is an evil caricature of the face of Christ.'

To believe in a vicarious sacrifice, is to think to take refuge with the Son from the righteousness of the Father; to take refuge with his work instead of with the Son himself; to take refuge with a theory of that work instead of the work itself; to shelter behind a false quirk of law instead of nestling in the eternal heart of the unchangeable and righteous Father, who is merciful in that he renders to every man according to his work, and compels their obedience, nor admits judicial quibble or subterfuge. God will never let a man off with any fault. He must have him clean. He will excuse him to the very uttermost of truth, but not a hair's-breadth beyond it; he is his true father, and will have his child true as his son Jesus Christ is true. He will impute to him nothing that he has not, will lose sight of no smallest good that he has; will quench no smoking flax, break no bruised reed, but send forth judgment unto victory. He is God beyond all that heart hungriest for love and righteousness could to eternity desire.

If you say the best of men have held the opinions I stigmatize, I answer, 'Some of the best of men have indeed held these theories, and of men who have held them I have loved and honoured some heartily and humbly—but because of what they *were*, not because of what they *thought*; and they were what they were in virtue of their obedient faith, not of their opinion. They were not better men because of holding these theories. In virtue of knowing God by obeying his son, they rose above the theories they had never looked in the face, and so had never recognized as evil. Many have arrived, in the natural progress of their sacred growth, at the point where they must abandon them. The man of whom I knew the most good gave them up gladly. Good to worshipfulness may be the man that holds them, and I hate them the more therefor; they are lies that, working under cover of the truth mingled with them, burrow as near the heart of the good man as they can go. Whoever, from whatever reason of blindness, may be the holder of a lie, the thing is a lie, and no falsehood must mingle with the justice we mete out to it. There is nothing for any lie but the pit of hell. Yet until the man sees the thing to be a lie, how shall he but hold it! Are there not mingled with it shadows of the best truth in the universe? So long as a man is able to love a lie, he is incapable of seeing it is a lie. He who is true, out and out, will know at once an untruth; and to that vision we must all come. I do not write for the sake of those who either make or heartily accept any lie. When they see the glory of God, they will see the eternal difference between the false and the true, and not till then. I write for those whom such teaching as theirs has folded in a cloud through which they cannot see the stars of heaven, so that some of them even doubt if there be any stars of heaven. For the holy ones who believed and taught these things in days gone by, all is well. Many of the holiest of them cast the lies from them long ere the present teachers of them were born. Many who would never have invented them for themselves, yet receiving them with the seals affixed of so many good men, took them in their humility as recognized truths, instead of inventions of men; and, oppressed by authority, the authority of men far inferior to themselves, did not dare dispute them, but proceeded to order their lives by what truths they found in their company, and so had their reward, the reward of obedience, in being by that obedience brought to know God, which knowledge broke for them the net of a presumptuous self-styled orthodoxy. Every man who tries to obey the Master is my brother, whether he counts me such or not, and I revere him; but dare I give quarter to what I see to be a lie, because my brother believes it? The lie is not of God, whoever may hold it.

'Well, then,' will many say, 'if you thus unceremoniously cast to the winds the doctrine of vicarious sacrifice, what theory do you propose to substitute in its stead?'

'In the name of the truth,' I answer, *None*. I will send out no theory of mine to rouse afresh little whirlwinds of dialogistic dust mixed with dirt and straws and holy words, hiding the Master in talk about him. If I have any such, I will not cast it on the road as I walk, but present it on a fair patine to him to whom I may think it well to show it. Only eyes opened by the sun of righteousness, and made single by obedience, can judge even the poor moony pearl of formulated thought. Say if you will that I fear to show my opinion. Is the man a coward who will not fling his child to the wolves? What faith in this kind I have, I will have to myself before God, till I see better reason for uttering it than I do now.

'Will you then take from me my faith, and help me to no other?'

Your faith! God forbid. Your theory is not your faith, nor anything like it. Your faith is your obedience; your theory I know not what. Yes, I will gladly leave you without any of what you call faith. Trust in God. Obey the word—every word of the Master. That is faith; and so believing, your opinion will grow out of your true life, and be worthy of it. Peter says the Lord gives the spirit to them that obey him: the spirit of the Master, and that alone, can guide you to any theory that it will be of use to you to hold. A theory arrived-at any other way is not worth the time spent on it. Jesus is the creating and saving lord of our intellects as well as of our more precious hearts; nothing that he does not think, is worth thinking; no man can think as he thinks, except he be pure like him; no man can be pure like him, except he go with him, and learn from him. To put off obeying him till we find a credible theory concerning him, is to set aside the potion we know it our duty to drink, for the study of the various schools of therapy. You know what Christ requires of you is right—much of it at least you believe to be right, and your duty to do, whether he said it or not: *do it.* If you do not do what you know of the truth, I do not wonder that you seek it intellectually, for that kind of search may well be, as Milton represents it, a solace even to the fallen angels. But do not call anything that may be so gained, *The Truth.* How can you, not caring to *be* true, judge concerning him whose life was to do for very love the things you confess your duty, yet do them not? Obey the truth, I say, and let theory wait. Theory may spring from life, but never life from theory.

I will not then tell you what I think, but I will

tell any man who cares to hear it what I believe. I will do it now. Of course what I say must partake thus much of the character of theory that I cannot prove it; I can only endeavour to order my life by it.

I believe in Jesus Christ, the eternal Son of God, my elder brother, my lord and master; I believe that he has a right to my absolute obedience whereinsoever I know or shall come to know his will; that to obey him is to ascend the pinnacle of my being; that not to obey him would be to deny him. I believe that he died that I might die like him—die to any ruling power in me but the will of God—live ready to be nailed to the cross as he was, if God will it. I believe that he is my Saviour from myself, and from all that has come of loving myself, from all that God does not love, and would not have me love—all that is not worth loving; that he died that the justice, the mercy of God, might have its way with me, making me just as God is just, merciful as he is merciful, perfect as my father in heaven is perfect. I believe and pray that he will give me what punishment I need to set me right, or keep me from going wrong. I believe that he died to deliver me from all meanness, all pretence, all falseness, all unfairness, all poverty of spirit, all cowardice, all fear, all anxiety, all forms of self-love, all trust or hope in possession; to make me merry as a child, the child of our father in heaven, loving nothing but what is lovely, desiring nothing I should be ashamed to let the universe of God see me desire. I believe that God is just like Jesus, only greater yet, for Jesus said so. I believe that God is absolutely, grandly beautiful, even as the highest soul of man counts beauty, but infinitely beyond that soul's highest idea—with the beauty that creates beauty, not merely shows it, or itself exists beautiful. I believe that God has always done, is always doing his best for every man; that no man is miserable because God is forgetting him; that he is not a God to crouch before, but our father, to whom the child-heart cries exultant, 'Do with me as thou wilt.'

I believe that there is nothing good for me or for any man but God, and more and more of God, and that alone through knowing Christ can we come nigh to him.

I believe that no man is ever condemned for any sin except one—that he will not leave his sins and come out of them, and be the child of him who is his father.

I believe that justice and mercy are simply one and the same thing; without justice to the full there can be no mercy, and without mercy to the full there can be no justice; that such is the mercy of God that he will hold his children in the consuming fire of his distance until they pay the uttermost farthing, until they drop the purse of selfishness with all the dross that is in it, and rush home to the Father and the Son, and the many brethren—rush inside the centre of the life-giving fire whose outer circles burn. I believe that no hell will be lacking which would help the just mercy of God to redeem his children.

I believe that to him who obeys, and thus opens the doors of his heart to receive the eternal gift, God gives the spirit of his son, the spirit of himself, to be in him, and lead him to the understanding of all truth; that the true disciple shall thus always know what he ought to do, though not necessarily what another ought to do; that the spirit of the father and the son enlightens by teaching righteousness. I believe that no teacher should strive to make men think as he thinks, but to lead them to the living Truth, to the Master himself, of whom alone they can learn anything, who will make them in themselves know what is true by the very seeing of it. I believe that the inspiration of the Almighty alone gives understanding. I believe that to be the disciple of Christ is the end of being; that to persuade men to be his disciples is the end of teaching.

'The sum of all this is that you do not believe in the atonement?'

I believe in Jesus Christ. Nowhere am I requested to believe *in* any thing, or *in* any statement, but everywhere to believe in God and in Jesus Christ. In what you call *the atonement*, in what you mean by the word, what I have already written must make it plain enough I do not believe. God forbid I should, for it would be to believe a lie, and a lie which is to blame for much non-acceptance of the gospel in this and other lands. But, as the word was used by the best English writers at the time when the translation of the Bible was made—with all my heart, and soul, and strength, and mind, I believe in the atonement, call it the *a-tone-ment*, or the *at-one-ment*, as you please. I believe that Jesus Christ *is* our atonement; that through him we are reconciled to, made one with God. There is not one word in the New Testament about reconciling God to us; it is we that have to be reconciled to God. I am not writing, neither desire to write, a treatise on the atonement, my business being to persuade men to be atoned to God; but I will go so far to meet my questioner as to say—without the slightest expectation of satisfying him, or the least care whether I do so or not, for his *opinion* is of no value to me, though his truth is of endless value to me and to the universe—that, even in the sense of the atonement being a making-up for the evil done by men toward God, I believe in the atonement. Did not the Lord cast himself into the eternal gulf of evil yawning between the children and the Father? Did he not bring the Father to us, let us look on our eternal Sire in the face of his true son, that we might have that in our hearts which alone could make us love him—a true sight of him? Did he not insist on the one truth of the universe, the one saving truth, that God was just what he was? Did he not hold to that assertion to the last, in the face of contradiction and death? Did he not thus lay down his life persuading us to lay down ours at the feet of the Father? Has not his very life by which he died passed into those who have received him, and re-created theirs, so that now they live with the life which alone is life? Did he not foil and slay evil by letting all the waves and billows of its horrid sea break upon him, go over him, and die without rebound—spend their rage, fall defeated, and cease? Verily, he made atonement! *We* sacrifice to God!—it is God who has sacrificed his own son to us; there was no way else of getting the gift of himself into our hearts. Jesus sacrificed himself to his father and the children to bring them together—all the love on the side of the Father and the Son, all the selfishness on the side of the children. If the joy that alone makes life worth living, the joy that God is such as Christ, be a true thing in my heart, how can I but believe in the atonement of Jesus Christ? I believe it heartily, as God means it.

Then again, as the power that brings about a making-up for any wrong done by man to man, I believe in the atonement. Who that believes in Jesus does not long to atone to his brother for the injury he has done him? What repentant child, feeling he has wronged his father, does not desire to make atonement? Who is the mover, the causer, the persuader, the creator of the repentance of the passion that restores fourfold?—Jesus, our propitiation, our atonement. He is the head and leader, the prince of the atonement. He could not do it without us, but he leads us up to the Father's knee: he makes us make atonement. Learning Christ, we are not only sorry for what we have done wrong, we not only turn from it and hate it, but we become able to serve both God and man with an infinitely high and true service, a soul-service. We are able to offer our whole being to God to whom by deepest right it belongs. Have I injured anyone? With him to aid my justice, new risen with him from the dead, shall I not make good amends? Have I failed in love to my neighbour? Shall I not now love him with an infinitely better love than was possible to me before? That I will and can make atonement, thanks be to him who is my atonement, making me at one with God and my fellows! He is my life, my joy, my lord, my owner, the perfecter of my being by the perfection of his own. I dare not say with Paul that I am the slave of Christ; but my highest aspiration and desire is to be the slave of Christ.

'But you do not believe that the sufferings of

Christ, as sufferings, justified the supreme ruler in doing anything which he would not have been at liberty to do but for those sufferings?'

I do not. I believe the notion as unworthy of man's belief, as it is dishonouring to God. It has its origin doubtless in a salutary sense of sin; but sense of sin is not inspiration, though it may lie not far from the temple-door. It is indeed an opener of the eyes, but upon home-defilement, not upon heavenly truth; it is not the revealer of secrets. Also there is another factor in the theory, and that is unbelief—incapacity to accept the freedom of God's forgiveness; incapacity to believe that it is God's chosen nature to forgive, that he is bound in his own divinely willed nature to forgive. No atonement is necessary to him but that men should leave their sins and come back to his heart. But men cannot believe in the forgiveness of God. Therefore they need, therefore he has given them a mediator. And yet they will not know him. They think of the father of souls as if he had abdicated his fatherhood for their sins, and assumed the judge. If he put off his fatherhood, which he cannot do, for it is an eternal fact, he puts off with it all relation to us. He cannot repudiate the essential and keep the resultant. Men cannot, or will not, or dare not see that nothing but his being our father gives him any right over us—that nothing but that could give him a perfect right. They regard the father of their spirits as their governor! They yield the idea of the Ancient of Days, 'the glad creator,' and put in its stead a miserable, puritanical martinet of a God, caring not for righteousness, but for his rights; not for the eternal purities, but the goody proprieties. The prophets of such a God take all the glow, all the hope, all the colour, all the worth, out of life on earth, and offer you instead what they call eternal bliss—a pale, tearless hell. Of all things, turn from a mean, poverty-stricken faith. But, if you are straitened in your own mammon-worshipping soul, how shall you believe in a God any greater than can stand up in that prison-chamber?

I desire to wake no dispute, will myself dispute with no man, but for the sake of those whom certain *believers* trouble, I have spoken my mind. I love the one God seen in the face of Jesus Christ. From all copies of Jonathan Edwards's portrait of God, however faded by time, however softened by the use of less glaring pigments, I turn with loathing. Not such a God is he concerning whom was the message John heard from Jesus, *that he is light, and in him is no darkness at all.*

LIGHT.

This then is the message which we have heard of him, and declare unto you, that God is light, and in him is no darkness at all.—1 *John* i. 5.

And this is the condemnation, that light is come into the world, and men loved darkness rather than light, because their deeds were evil.—*John* iii. 19.

WE call the story of Jesus, told so differently, yet to my mind so consistently, by four narrators, *the gospel*. What makes this tale *the good news*? Is everything in the story of Christ's life on earth good news? Is it good news that the one only good man was served by his fellow-men as Jesus was served —cast out of the world in torture and shame? Is it good news that he came to his own, and his own received him not? What makes it fit, I repeat, to call the tale *good news*? If we asked this or that theologian, we should, in so far as he was a true man, and answered from his own heart and not from the tradition of the elders, understand what he saw in it that made it good news to him, though it might involve what would be anything but good news to some of us. The deliverance it might seem to this or that man to bring, might be founded on such notions of God as to not a few of us contain as little of good as of news. To share in the deliverance which some men find in what they call the gospel—for all do not apply the word to the tale itself, but to certain deductions made from the epistles and their own consciousness of evil—we should have to believe such things of God as would be the opposite of an evangel to us—yea, a message from hell itself; we should have to imagine that whose possibility would be worse than any ill from which their 'good news' might offer us deliverance: we must first believe in an unjust God, from whom we have to seek refuge. True, they call him just, but say he does that which seems to the best in me the essence of injustice. They will tell me I judge after the flesh: I answer, Is it then to the flesh the Lord appeals when he says, 'Yea, and why even of yourselves judge ye not what is right?' Is he not the light that lighteth every man that cometh into the world? They tell me I was born in sin, and I know it to be true; they tell me also that I am judged with the same severity as if I had been born in righteousness, and that I know to be false. They make it a consequence of the purity and justice of God that he will judge us, born in evil, for which birth we were not accountable, by our sinfulness, instead of by our guilt. They tell me, or at least give me to understand, that every wrong thing I have done makes me subject to be treated as if I had done that thing with the free will of one who had in him no taint of evil—when, perhaps, I did not at the time recognize the thing as evil, or recognized it only in the vaguest fashion. Is there any gospel in telling me that God is unjust, but that there is a way of deliverance from him? Show me my God unjust, and you wake in me a damnation from which no power can deliver me—least of all God himself. It may be good news to such as are content to have a God capable of unrighteousness, if only he be on their side!

Who would not rejoice to hear from Matthew, or Mark, or Luke, what, in a few words, he meant by the word *gospel*—or rather, what in the story of Jesus made him call it *good news*! Each would probably give a different answer to the question, all the answers consistent, and each a germ from which the others might be reasoned; but in the case of John, we have his answer to the question: he gives us in one sentence of two members, not indeed the gospel according to John, but the gospel according to Jesus Christ himself. He had often told the story of Jesus, the good news of what he was, and did, and said: what in it all did John look upon as the essence of the goodness of its news? In his gospel he gives us all *about* him, the message *concerning* him; now he tells us what in it makes it to himself and to us good news—tells us the very goodness of the good news. It is not now his own message about Jesus, but the soul of that message—that which makes it gospel—the news Jesus brought concerning the Father, and gave to the disciples as his message for them to deliver to men. Throughout the story, Jesus, in all he does, and is, and says, is telling the news concerning his father, which he was sent to give to John and his companions, that they might hand it on to their brothers; but here, in so many words, John tells us what he himself has heard from The Word— what in sum he has gathered from Jesus as the message he has to declare He has received it in no systematic form; it is what a life, *the* life, what a man, *the* man, has taught him. The Word is the Lord; the Lord is the gospel. The good news is no fagot of sticks of a man's gathering on the Sabbath.

Every man must read the Word for himself. One may read it in one shape, another in another: all will be right if it be indeed the Word they read, and they read it by the lamp of obedience. He who is willing to do the will of the Father shall know the truth of the teaching of Jesus. The spirit is 'given to them that obey him.'

But let us hear how John reads the Word— hear what is John's version of the gospel.

'This then is the message,' he says, 'which we have heard of him, and declare unto you, that God is light, and in him is no darkness at all.' Ah, my heart, this is indeed the good news for thee! This *is* a gospel! If God be light, what more, what else can I seek than God, than God himself! Away with your doctrines! Away with your salvation from the 'justice' of a God whom it is a horror to imagine! Away with your iron cages of false metaphysics! I am saved—for God is light! My God, I come to thee. That thou shouldst be thyself is enough for time and eternity, for my soul and all its endless need. Whatever seems to me darkness, that I will not believe of my God. If I should mistake, and call that darkness which is light, will he not reveal the matter to me, setting it in the light that lighteth every man, showing me that I saw but the husk of the thing, not the kernel? Will he not break open the shell for me, and let the truth of it, his thought, stream out upon me? He will not let it hurt me to mistake the light for darkness, while I take not the darkness for light. The one comes from blindness of the intellect, the other from blindness of heart and will. I love the light, and will not believe at the word of any man, or upon the conviction of any man, that that which seems to me darkness is in God. Where would the good news be if John said, 'God is light, but you cannot see his light; you cannot tell, you have no notion, what light is; what God means by light, is not what you mean by light; what God calls light may be horrible darkness to you, for you are of another nature from him!' Where, I say, would be the good news of that? It is true, the light of God may be so bright that we see nothing; but that is not darkness, it is infinite hope of light. It is true also that to the wicked 'the day of the Lord is darkness, and not light;' but is that because the conscience of the wicked man judges of good and evil oppositely to the conscience of the good man? When he says, 'Evil, be thou my good,' he means by *evil* what God means by evil, and by *good* he means *pleasure*. He cannot make the meanings change places. To say that what our deepest conscience calls darkness may be light to God, is blasphemy; to say light in God and light in man are of differing kinds, is to speak against the spirit of light. God is light far beyond what we can see, but what we mean by light, God means by light; and what is light to God is light to us, or would be light to us if we saw it, and will be light to us when we do see it. God means us to be jubilant in the fact that he is light—that he is what his children, made in his image, mean when they say *light*; that what in him is dark to them, is dark by excellent glory, by too much cause of jubilation; that, however dark it may be to their eyes, it is light even as they mean it, light for their eyes and souls and hearts to take in the moment they are enough of eyes, enough of souls, enough of hearts, to receive it in its very being. Living Light, thou wilt not have me believe anything dark of thee! thou wilt have me so sure of thee as to dare to say that is not of God which I see dark, see unlike the Master! If I am not honest enough, if the eye in me be not single enough to see thy light, thou wilt punish me, I thank thee, and purge my eyes from their darkness, that they may let the light in, and so I become an inheritor, with thy other children, of that light which is thy Godhead, and makes thy creatures need to worship thee. ' In thy light we shall see light.'

All men will not, in our present imperfection, see the same light; but light is light notwithstanding, and what each does see, is his safety if he obeys it. In proportion as we have the image of Christ mirrored in us, we shall know what is and is not light. But never will anything prove to be light that is not of the same kind with that which we mean by light, with that in a thing which makes us call it light. The darkness yet left in us makes us sometimes doubt of a thing whether it be light or darkness; but when the eye is single, the whole body will be full of light.

To fear the light is to be untrue, or at least it comes of untruth. No being, for himself or for another, needs fear the light of God. Nothing can be in light inimical to our nature, which is of God, or to anything in us that is worthy. All fear of the light, all dread lest there should be something dangerous in it, comes of the darkness still in those of us who do not love the truth with all our hearts; it will vanish as we are more and more interpenetrated with the light. In a word, there is no way of thought or action which we count admirable in man, in which God is not altogether adorable. There is no loveliness, nothing that makes man dear to his brother man, that is not in God, only it is infinitely better in God. He is God our saviour. Jesus is our saviour because God is our saviour. He is the God of comfort and consolation. He will soothe and satisfy his children better than any mother her infant. The only thing he will not give them is—leave to stay in the dark. If a child cry, 'I want the darkness,' and complain that he will not give it, yet he will not give it. He gives what his child needs—often by refusing what he asks. If his child say, 'I will not be good; I prefer to die; let me die!' his dealing with that child will be as if he said—'No; I have the right to content you, not giving you your own will but mine, which is your one good. You shall not die; you shall live to thank me that I would not hear your prayer. You know what you ask, but not what you refuse.' There are good things God must delay giving until his child has a pocket to hold them—till he gets his child to make that pocket. He must first make him fit to receive and to have. There is no part of our nature that shall not be satisfied—and that not by lessening it, but by enlarging it to embrace an ever-enlarging enough.

Come to God, then, my brother, my sister, with all thy desires and instincts, all thy lofty ideals, all thy longing for purity and unselfishness, all thy yearning to love and be true, all thy aspirations after self-forgetfulness and child-life in the breath of the Father; come to him with all thy weaknesses, all thy shames, all thy futilities; with all thy helplessness over thy own thoughts; with all thy failure, yea, with the sick sense of having missed the tide of true affairs; come to him with all thy doubts, fears, dishonesties, meannesses, paltrinesses, misjudgments, wearinesses, disappointments, and stalenesses: be sure he will take thee and all thy miserable brood, whether of dragglewinged angels, or covert-seeking snakes, into his care, the angels for life, the snakes for death, and thee for liberty in his limitless heart! For he is light, and in him is no darkness at all. If he were a king, a governor; if the name that described him were *The Almighty*, thou mightst well doubt whether there could be light enough in him for thee and thy darkness; but he is thy father, and more thy father than the word can mean in any lips but his who said, ' my father and your father, my God and your God;' and such a father *is* light, an infinite, perfect light. If he were any less or any other than he is, and thou couldst yet go on growing, thou must at length come to the point where thou wouldst be dissatisfied with him; but he is light, and in him is no darkness at all. If anything seem to be in him that you cannot be content with, be sure that the ripening of thy love to thy fellows and to him, the source of thy being, will make thee at length know that anything else than just what he is would have been to thee an endless loss. Be not afraid to build upon the rock Christ, as if thy holy imagination might build too high and heavy for that rock, and it must give way and crumble beneath the weight of thy divine idea. Let no one persuade thee that there is in him a little darkness, because of something he has said which his creature interprets into darkness. The interpretation is the work of the enemy—a handful of tares of darkness sown in the light. Neither let thy cowardly conscience receive any word as light because another calls it light, while it looks to thee dark. Say either the thing is not what it seems, or God never said or did it. But, of all evils, to misinterpret what God does, and then say the thing as interpreted must be right because God does it, is of the devil. Do not try to believe anything that affects thee as darkness. Even if thou mistake and refuse something true thereby, thou wilt do less wrong to Christ by such a refusal than thou wouldst by accepting as his what thou canst see only as darkness. It is impossible thou art seeing a true, a real thing—seeing it as it is, I mean—if it looks to thee darkness. But let thy words be few, lest thou say with thy tongue what thou wilt afterward repent with thy heart. Above all things believe in the light, that it is what thou callest light, though the darkness in thee may give thee cause at a time to doubt whether thou art verily seeing the light.

'But there is another side to the matter: God is light indeed, but there *is* darkness; darkness is death, and men are in it.'

Yes; darkness is death, but not death to him that comes out of it.

It may sound paradoxical, but no man is condemned for anything he has done; he is condemned for continuing to do wrong. He is condemned for not coming out of the darkness, for not coming to the light, the living God, who sent the light, his son, into the world to guide him home. Let us hear what John says about the darkness.

For here also we have, I think, the word of the apostle himself: at the 13th verse he begins, I think, to speak in his own person. In the 19th verse he says, 'And this is the condemnation,'— not that men are sinners—not that they have done that which, even at the moment, they were ashamed of—not that they have committed murder, not that they have betrayed man or woman, not that they have ground the faces of the poor, making money by the groans of their fellows—not for any hideous thing are they condemned, but that they will not leave such doings behind, and do them no more: 'This is the condemnation, that light is come into the world, and men' would not come out of the darkness to the light, but 'loved darkness rather than light, because their deeds were evil.' Choosing evil, clinging to evil, loving the darkness because it suits with their deeds, therefore turning their backs on the inbreaking light, how can they but be condemned—if God be true, if he be light, and darkness be alien to him! Whatever of honesty is in man, whatever of judgment is left in the world, must allow that their condemnation is in the very nature of things, that it must rest on them and abide.

But if one happens to utter some individual truth which another man has made into one of the cogs of his system, he is in danger of being supposed to accept all the toothed wheels and their relations in that system. I therefore go on to say that it does not follow, because light has come into the world, that it has fallen upon this or that man. He has his portion of the light that lighteth every man, but the revelation of God in Christ may not yet have reached him. A man might see and pass the Lord in a crowd, nor be to blame like the Jews of Jerusalem for not knowing him. A man like Nathanael might have started and stopped at the merest glimpse of him, but all growing men are not yet like him without guile. Everyone who has not yet come to the light is not necessarily keeping his face turned away from it. We dare not say that this or that man would not have come to the light had he seen it ; we do not know that he will not come to the light the moment he does see it. God gives every man time. There is a light that lightens sage and savage, but the glory of God in the face of Jesus may not have shined on this sage or that savage. The condemnation is of those who, having seen Jesus, refuse to come to him, or pretend to come to him but do not the things he says. They have all sorts of excuses at hand ; but as soon as a man begins to make excuse, the time has come when he might be doing that from which he excuses himself. How many are there not who, believing there is something somewhere with the claim of light upon them, go on and on to get more out of the darkness ! This consciousness, all neglected by them, gives broad ground for the expostulation of the Lord —'Ye will not come unto me that ye might have life !'

'All manner of sin and blasphemy,' the Lord said, 'shall be forgiven unto men ; but the blasphemy against the spirit shall not be forgiven.' God speaks, as it were, in this manner : ' I forgive you everything. Not a word more shall be said about your sins—only come out of them; come out of the darkness of your exile; come into the light of your home, of your birthright, and do evil no more. Lie no more; cheat no more; oppress no more; slander no more; envy no more; be neither greedy nor vain; love your neighbour as I love you; be my good child; trust in your father. I am light; come to me, and you shall see things as I see them, and hate the evil thing. I will make you love the thing which now you call good and love not. I forgive all the past.'

'I thank thee, Lord, for forgiving me, but I prefer staying in the darkness: forgive me that too.'

'No; that cannot be. The one thing that cannot be forgiven is the sin of choosing to be evil, of refusing deliverance. It is impossible to forgive that sin. It would be to take part in it. To side with wrong against right, with murder against life, cannot be forgiven. The thing that is past I pass, but he who goes on doing the same, annihilates this my forgiveness, makes it of no effect. Let a man have committed any sin whatever, I forgive him; but to choose to go on sinning—how can I forgive that? It would be to nourish and cherish evil! It would be to let my creation go to ruin. Shall I keep you alive to do things hateful in the sight of all true men? If a man refuse to come out of his sin, he must suffer the vengeance of a love that would be no love if it left him there. Shall I allow my creature to be the thing my soul hates?'

There is no excuse for this refusal. If we were punished for every fault, there would be no end, no respite; we should have no quiet wherein to repent; but God passes by all he can. He passes by and forgets a thousand sins, yea, tens of thousands, forgiving them all—only we must begin to be good, begin to do evil no more. He who refuses must be punished and punished—punished through all the ages—punished until he gives way, yields, and comes to the light, that his deeds may be seen by himself to be what they are, and be by himself reproved, and the Father at last have his child again. For the man who in this world resists to the full, there may be, perhaps, a whole age or era in the history of the universe during which his sin shal not be forgiven; but *never* can it be forgiven until he repents. How can they who will not repent be forgiven, save in the sense that God does and will do all he can to make them repent? Who knows but such sin may need for its cure the continuous punishment of an æon?

There are three conceivable kinds of punishment—first, that of mere retribution, which I take to be entirely and only human—therefore, indeed, more properly inhuman, for that which is not divine is not essential to humanity, and is of evil, and an intrusion upon the human; second, that which works repentance; and third, that which refines and purifies, working for holiness. But the punishment that falls on whom the Lord loveth because they have repented, is a very different thing from the punishment that falls on those whom he loveth indeed but cannot forgive because they hold fast by their sins.

There are also various ways in which the word *forgive* can be used. A man might say to his son—'My boy, I forgive you. You did not know what you were doing. I will say no more about it.' Or he might say—'My boy, I forgive you; but I must punish you, for you have done the same thing several times, and I must make you remember.' Or, again, he might say—'I am seriously angry with you. I cannot forgive you. I must punish

you severely. The thing was too shameful! I cannot pass it by.' Or, once more, he might say—
'Except you alter your ways entirely, I shall have nothing more to do with you. You need not come to me. I will not take the responsibility of anything you do. So far from answering for you, I shall feel bound in honesty to warn my friends not to put confidence in you. Never, never, till I see a greater difference in you than I dare hope to see in this world, will I forgive you. I can no more regard you as one of the family. I would die to save you, but I cannot forgive you. There is nothing in you now on which to rest forgiveness. To say, I forgive you, would be to say, Do anything you like; I do not care what you do.' So God may forgive and punish; and he may punish and not forgive, that he may rescue. To forgive the sin against the holy spirit would be to damn the universe to the pit of lies, to render it impossible for the man so forgiven ever to be saved. He cannot forgive the man who will not come to the light because his deeds are evil. Against that man his fatherly heart is *moved with indignation*.

THE DISPLEASURE OF JESUS.

When Jesus therefore saw her weeping, and the Jews also weeping which came with her, he groaned in the spirit, and was troubled.—*John* xi. 33.

GRIMM, in his lexicon to the New Testament, after giving as the equivalent of the word ἐμβριμάομαι in pagan use, 'I am moved with anger,' 'I roar or growl,' 'I snort at,' 'I am vehemently angry or indignant with some one,' tells us that in Mark i. 43, and Matthew ix. 30, it has a meaning different from that of the pagans, namely, 'I command with severe admonishment.' That he has any authority for saying so, I do not imagine, and believe the statement a blunder. The Translators and Revisers, however, have in those passages used the word similarly, and in one place, the passage before us, where a true version is of yet more consequence, have taken another liberty and rendered the word 'groaned.' The Revisers, at the same time, place in the margin what I cannot but believe its true meaning—'was moved with indignation.'

Let us look at all the passages in which the word is used of the Lord, and so, if we may, learn something concerning him. The only place in the gospel where it is used of any but the Lord is Mark xiv. 5. Here both versions say of the disciples that they 'murmured at' the waste of the ointment by one of the women who anointed the Lord. With regard to this rendering I need only remark that surely 'murmured at' can hardly be strong enough, especially seeing 'they had indignation among themselves' at the action.

It is indeed right and necessary to insist that many a word must differ in moral weight and colour as used of or by persons of different character. The anger of a good man is a very different thing from the anger of a bad man; the displeasure of Jesus must be a very different thing from the displeasure of a tyrant. But they are both anger, both displeasure, nevertheless. We have no right to change a root-meaning, and say in one case that a word means *he was indignant*, in another that it means *he straitly or strictly charged*, and in a third that it means *he groaned*. Surely not thus shall we arrive at the truth! If any statement is made, any word employed, that we feel unworthy of the Lord, let us refuse it; let us say, 'I do not believe that;' or, 'There must be something there that I cannot see into': I must wait; it cannot be what it looks to me, and be true of the Lord!' But to accept the word as used of the Lord, and say it means something quite different from what it means when used by the same writer of some one else, appears to me untruthful.

We shall take first the passage, Mark i. 43—in the authorized version, 'And he straitly charged him;' in the revised, 'And he strictly charged him,' with '*sternly*' in the margin. Literally, as it seems to me, it reads, and ought to be read, 'And being angry' or 'displeased' or 'vexed' 'with him, he immediately dismissed him.' There is even some dissatisfaction implied, I think, in the word I have translated 'dismissed.' The word in John ix. 34, 'they cast him out,' is the same, only a little intensified.

This adds something to the story, and raises the question, Why should Jesus have been angry? If we can find no reason for his anger, we must leave the thing as altogether obscure; for I do not know where to find another meaning for the word, except in the despair of a would-be interpreter.

Jesus had cured the leper—not with his word only, which would have been enough for the mere cure, but was not enough without the touch of his hand—the Sinaitic version says 'his *hands*'—to satisfy the heart of Jesus—a touch defiling him, in the notion of the Jew, but how cleansing to the sense of the leper! The man, however, seems to have been unworthy of this delicacy of divine tenderness. The Lord, who could read his heart, saw that he made him no true response—that there was not awaked in him the faith he desired to rouse: he had not drawn the soul of the man to his. The leper was jubilant in the removal of his pain and isolating uncleanness, in his deliverance from suffering and scorn; he was probably elated with the pride of having had a miracle wrought for *him*. In a word, he was so full of himself that he did not think truly of his deliverer.

The Lord, I say, saw this, or something of this kind, and was not satisfied. He had wanted to give the man something so much better than a pure skin, and had only roused in him an unseemly delight in his own cleanness—*unseemly*, for it was such that he paid no heed to the Lord, but immediately disobeyed his positive command. The moral position the man took was that which displeased the Lord, made him angry. He saw in him positive and rampant self-will and disobedience, an impertinent assurance and self-satisfaction. Filled, not with pure delight, or the child-like merriment that might well burst forth, mingled with tears, at such deliverance; filled, not with gratitude, but gratification, the keener that he had been so long an object of loathing to his people; filled with arrogance because of the favour shown to him, of all men, by the great prophet, and swelling with boast of the same, he left the presence of the healer to thwart his will, and, commanded to tell no man, at once 'began'—the frothy, volatile, talking soul—'to publish it much, and to blaze abroad the matter, insomuch that Jesus could no more openly enter into a city, but was without in desert places.'

Let us next look at the account of the healing of the two blind men, given in the ninth chapter of Matthew's gospel. In both the versions the same phrases are used in translation of the word in ques-

tion, as in the story of the leper in Mark's gospel—
'straitly,' 'strictly,' 'sternly charged them.' I read
the passage thus : 'And Jesus was displeased '—or,
perhaps, ' much displeased '—' with them, saying,
See that no man know it.'

' But they went forth, and spread abroad his
fame in all that land.' Surely here we have light
on the cause of Jesus' displeasure with the blind
men ! it was the same with them as with the leper :
they showed themselves bent on their own way,
and did not care for his. Doubtless they were, in
part, all of them moved by the desire to spread
abroad his fame ; that may even have seemed to
them the best acknowledgment they could render
their deliverer. They never suspected that a great
man might desire to avoid fame, laying no value
upon it, knowing it for a foolish thing. They did
not understand that a man desirous of helping his
fellows might yet avoid a crowd as obstructive to
his object. 'What is a prophet without honour ? '
such virtually ask, nor understand the answer, ' A
man the more likely to prove a prophet.' These
men would repay their healer with trumpeting, not
obedience. By them he should have his right—but
as they not he judged fit ! In his modesty he

objected, but they would take care he should not go without his reward! Through them he should reap the praises of men! 'Not tell!' they exclaim. 'Indeed, we will tell!' They were too grateful not to rumour him, not grateful enough to obey him.

We cannot surely be amazed at their self-sufficiency. How many are there not who seem capable of anything for the sake of the church or Christianity, except the one thing its Lord cares about—that they should do what he tells them! He would deliver them from themselves into the liberty of the sons of God, make them his brothers; they leave him to vaunt their church. His commandments are not grievous; they invent commandments for him, and lay them, burdens grievous to be borne, upon the necks of their brethren. God would have us sharers in his bliss—in the very truth of existence; they worship from afar, and will not draw nigh. It was not, I think, the obstruction to his work, not the personal inconvenience it would cause him, that made the Lord angry, but that they would not be his friends, would not do what he told them, would not be the children of his father, and help him to save their brethren. When Peter in his way next—much the same way as theirs—opposed the will of the Father, saying, 'That be far from thee, Lord!' he called him Satan, and ordered him behind him.

Does it affect anyone to the lowering of his idea of the Master that he should ever be angry? If so, I would ask him whether his whole conscious experience of anger be such, that he knows but one kind of anger. There is a good anger and a bad anger. There is a wrath of God, and there is a wrath of man that worketh not the righteousness of God. Anger may be as varied as the colour of the rainbow. God's anger can be nothing but Godlike, therefore divinely beautiful, at one with his love, helpful, healing, restoring; yet is it verily and truly what we call anger. How different is the anger of one who loves, from that of one who hates! yet is anger anger. There is the degraded human anger, and the grand, noble, eternal anger. Our anger is in general degrading, because it is in general impure.

It is to me an especially glad thought that the Lord came so near us as to be angry with us. The more we think of Jesus being angry with us, the more we feel that we must get nearer and nearer to him—get within the circle of his wrath, out of the sin that makes him angry, and near to him where sin cannot come. There is no quenching of his love in the anger of Jesus. The anger of Jesus is his recognition that we are to blame; if we were not to blame, Jesus could never be angry with us; we should not be of his kind, therefore not subject to his blame. To recognize that we are to blame, is to say that we ought to be better, that we are able to do right if we will. We are able to turn our faces to the light, and come out of the darkness; the Lord will see to our growth.

It is a serious thought that the disobedience of the men he had set free from blindness and leprosy should be able to hamper him in his work for his father. But his best friends, his lovers did the same. That he should be crucified was a horror to them; they would have made him a king, and ruined his father's work. He preferred the cruelty of his enemies to the kindness of his friends. The former with evil intent wrought his father's will; the latter with good intent would have frustrated it. His disciples troubled him with their unbelieving expostulations. Let us know that the poverty of our idea of Jesus—how much more our disobedience to him!—thwarts his progress to victory, delays the coming of the kingdom of heaven. Many a man valiant for Christ, but not understanding him, and laying on himself and his fellows burdens against nature, has therein done will-worship and would-be service for which Christ will give him little thanks, which indeed may now be moving his holy anger. Where we do that we ought not, and could have helped it, be moved to anger against us, O Christ! do not treat us as if we were not worth being displeased with; let not our faults pass as if they were of no weight. Be angry with us, holy brother, wherein we are to blame; where we do not understand, have patience with us, and open our eyes, and give us strength to obey, until at length we are the children of the Father even as thou. For though thou art lord and master and saviour of them that are growing, thou art perfect lord only of the true and the safe and the free, who live in thy light and are divinely glad: we keep thee back from thy perfect lordship. Make us able to be angry and not sin; to be angry nor seek revenge the smallest; to be angry and full of forgiveness. We will not be content till our very anger is love.

The Lord did not call the leprosy to return and seize again upon the man who disobeyed him. He may have deserved it, but the Lord did not do it. He did not wrap the self-confident seeing men in the cloud of their old darkness because they wrapped themselves in the cloud of disobedience. He let them go. Of course they failed of their well-being by it; for to say a man might disobey and be none the worse, would be to say that *no* may be *yes*, and light sometimes darkness; it would be to say that the will of God is not man's bliss. But the Lord did not directly punish them, any more than he does tens of thousands of wrongs in the world. Many wrongs punish themselves against the bosses of armed law; many wrong-doers cut themselves, like the priests of Baal, with the knives of their own injustice; and it is his will it should be so; but, whether he punish directly or indirectly, he is always working to deliver. I think sometimes his anger is followed, yea, accompanied by an astounding gift, fresh from his heart of grace. He knows what to do, for he is love. He is love when he gives, and love when he withholds; love when he heals, and love when he slays. Lord, if thus thou lookest upon men in thine anger, what must a full gaze be from thine eyes of love!

The Displeasure of Jesus

Let us now look at the last case in which this word ἐμβριμάομαι is used in the story of our Lord—that form of it, at least, which we have down here, for sure they have a fuller gospel in the Father's house, and without spot of blunder in it: let us so use that we have that we be allowed at length to look within the leaves of the other!

In the authorized version of the gospel of John, the eleventh chapter, the thirty-third verse, we have the words: 'When Jesus therefore saw her weeping, and the Jews also weeping which came with her, he groaned in the spirit and was troubled;' —according to the margin of the revised version, 'he was moved with indignation in the spirit, and troubled himself.' Also in the thirty-eighth verse we read, according to the margin of the revised version, 'Jesus therefore again being moved with indignation in himself cometh to the tomb.'

Indignation—anger at the very tomb! in the presence of hearts torn by the loss of a brother four days dead, whom also he loved! Yes, verily, friends! such indignation, such anger as, at such a time, in such a place, it was eternally right the heart of Jesus should be moved withal. I can hardly doubt that he is in like manner moved by what he sees now at the death-beds and graves of not a few who are not his enemies, and yet in the presence of death seem no better than pagans. What have such gained by being the Christians they say they are? They fix their eyes on a grisly phantasm they call Death, and never lift them to the radiant Christ standing by bed or grave! For them Christ has not conquered Death:

> Thou art our king, O Death! to thee we groan!

They would shudder at the thought of saying so in words; they say it in the bitterness of their tears, in their eyes of despair, in their black garments, in their instant retreat from the light of day to burrow in the bosom of darkness? 'What, would you have us not weep?' Weep freely, friends; but let your tears be those of expectant Christians, not hopeless pagans. Let us look at the story.

The Lord had all this time been trying to teach his friends about his father—what a blessed and perfect father he was, who had sent him that men might look on his very likeness, and know him greater than any likeness could show him;

and all they had gained by it seemed not to amount to an atom of consolation when the touch of death came. He had said hundreds of things to Martha and Mary that are not down in the few pages of our earthly gospel; but the fact that God loves them, and that God has Lazarus, seems nothing to them because they have not Lazarus! The Lord himself, for all he has been to them, cannot console them, even with his bodily presence, for the bodily absence of their brother. I do not mean that God would have even his closest presence make us forget or cease to desire that of our friend. God forbid! The love of God is the perfecting of every love. He is not the God of oblivion, but of eternal remembrance. There is no past with him. So far is he from such jealousy as we have all heard imputed to him, his determination is that his sons and daughters shall love each other perfectly. He gave us to each other to belong to each other for ever. He does not give to take away; with him is no variableness or shadow of turning. But if my son or daughter be gone from me for a season, should not the coming of their mother comfort me? Is it nothing that he who is the life should be present, assuring the well-being of the life that has vanished, and the well-being of the love that misses it? Why should the Lord have come to the world at all, if these his friends were to take no more good of him than this? Having the elder brother, could they not do for a little while without the younger? Must they be absolutely miserable without him? All their cry was, 'Lord, if thou hadst been here, my brother had not died!' You may say they did not know Christ well enough yet. That is plain —but Christ had expected more of them, and was disappointed. You may say, 'How could that be, seeing he knew what was in man?' I doubt if you think rightly how much the Lord gave up in coming to us. Perhaps you have a poor idea of how much the Son was able to part with, or rather could let the Father take from him, without his sonship, the eternal to the eternal, being touched by it, save to show it deeper and deeper, closer and closer. That he did not in this world know everything, is plain from his own words, and from signs as well: I should scorn to imagine that ignorance touching his Godhead, that his Godhead could be hurt by what enhances his devotion. It enhances in my eyes the idea of his Godhead.

Here, I repeat, I cannot but think that he was disappointed with his friends Martha and Mary. Had he done no more for them than this? Was his father and their father no comfort to them? Was this the way his best friends treated his father, who was doing everything for them possible for a father to do for his children! He cared so dearly for their hearts that he could not endure to see them weeping so that they shut out his father. His love was vexed with them that they would sit in ashes when they ought to be out in his father's sun and wind. And all for a lie!—since the feeling in their hearts that made them so weep, was a false one. Remember, it was not their love, but a false notion of loss. Were they no nearer the light of life than that? To think they should believe in death and the grave, not in him, the Life! Why should death trouble them? Why grudge the friendly elements their grasp on the body, restoring it whence it came, because Lazarus was gone home to God, and needed it no more? I suspect that, looking into their hearts, he saw them feeling and acting just as if Lazarus had ceased to exist.

'Lord, if thou hadst been here, my brother had

not died. But I know, that even now, whatsoever thou wilt ask of God, God will give it thee.'

'Thy brother shall rise again.'

'I know that he shall rise again in the resurrection at the last day.'

'I am the resurrection, and the life: he that believeth in me, though he were dead, yet shall he live. And whosoever liveth, and believeth in me, shall never die.'

I will not now endeavour to disclose anything of the depth of this word of the Lord. It will suffice for my present object to say that the sisters must surely have known that he raised up the daughter of Jairus and the son of the widow of Nain; and if the words he had just spoken, 'Thy brother shall rise again,' seemed to Martha too good to be true in the sense that he was going to raise him now, both she and Mary believing he could raise him if he would, might at least have known that if he did not, it must be for reasons as lovely as any for which he might have done it. If he could, and did not, must it not be as well as, yes, better than if he did?

Martha had gone away, for the moment at least, a little comforted; and now came Mary, who knew the Lord better than her sister—alas, with the same bitter tears flowing from her eyes, and the same hopeless words, almost of reproach, falling from her lips! Then it was—at the sight of her and the Jews with her weeping, that the spirit of the Lord was moved with indignation. They wept as those who believe in death, not in life. Mary wept as if she had never seen with her eyes, never handled with her hands the Word of life! He was troubled with their unbelief, and troubled with their trouble. What was to be done with his brothers and sisters who *would* be miserable, who would not believe in his father! What a life of pain was theirs! How was he to comfort them? They would not be comforted! What a world was it that would go on thus—that would not free itself from the clutch of death, even after death was dead, but would weep and weep for thousands of years to come, clasped to the bosom of dead Death! Was existence, the glorious outgift of his father, to be the most terrible of miseries, because some must go home before others? It was all so sad!—and all because they would not know his father! Then came the reaction from his indignation, and the labouring heart of the Lord found relief in tears.

The Lord was standing, as it were, on the watershed of life. On one side of him lay what Martha and Mary called the world of life, on the other what he and his father and Lazarus called more abundant life. The Lord saw into both worlds—saw Martha and Mary on the one side weeping, on the other Lazarus waiting for them in peace. He would do his best for them—for the sisters—not for Lazarus! It was hard on Lazarus to be called back into the winding-sheet of the body, a sacrifice to their faithlessness, but it should be done! Lazarus should suffer for his sisters! Through him they should be compelled to believe in the Father, and so be delivered from bondage! Death should have no more dominion over them!

He was vexed with them, I have said, for not believing in God, his and their father; and at the same time was troubled with their trouble. The cloud of his loving anger and disappointed sympathy broke in tears; and the tears eased his heart of the weight of its divine grief. He turned, not to them, not to punish them for their unbelief, not even to chide them for their sorrow; he turned to his father to thank him.

He thanks him for hearing a prayer he had made—whether a moment before, or ere he left the other side of the Jordan, I cannot tell. What was the prayer for having heard which he now thanks his father? Surely he had spoken about bringing Lazarus back, and his father had shown himself of one mind with him. 'And I knew that thou hearest me always, but because of the multitude which standeth around I said it, that they may believe that thou didst send me.' 'I said it:' said what? He had said something for the sake of the multitude; what was it? The thanksgiving he had just uttered. He was not in the way of thanking his father in formal words; and now would not naturally have spoken his thanks aloud; for he was always speaking to the Father, and the Father was always hearing him; but he had a reason for doing so, and was now going to give his reason. He had done the unusual thing for the sake of being heard do it, and for holy honesty-sake he tells the fact, speaking to his father so as the people about him may hear, and there be no shadow of undisclosed doubleness in the action —nothing covert, however perfect in honesty. His design in thus thanking aloud must be made patent!

'I thank thee, father, for hearing me; and I say it, not as if I had had any doubt of thy hearing me, but that the people may understand that I am not doing this thing of myself, but as thy messenger. It is thou, father, art. going to do it; I am doing it as thy right hand.—Lazarus, come forth.'

I have said the trouble of the Lord was that his friends would not trust his father. He did not want any reception of himself that was not a reception of his father. It was his father, not he, that did the works! From this disappointment came, it seems to me, that sorrowful sigh, 'Nevertheless, when the son of man cometh, shall he find faith on the earth?'

The thought of the Lord in uttering this prayer is not his own justification, but his father's reception by his children. If ever the Lord claims to be received as a true man, it is for the sake of his father and his brethren, that in the receiving of him, he may be received who sent him. Had he now desired the justification of his own claim, the thing he was about to do would have been powerful to that end; but he must have them understand clearly that the Father was one with him in it—

that they were doing it together—that it was the will of the Father—that he had sent him.

Lazarus must come and help him with these sisters whom he could not get to believe! Lazarus had tasted of death, and knew what it was: he must come and give his testimony! 'They have lost sight of you, Lazarus, and fancy you gone to the nowhere of their unbelief. Come forth; come out of the unseen. We will set them at rest.' It was hard, I repeat, upon Lazarus; he was better where he was; but he must come and bear the Lord company a little longer, and then be left behind with his sisters, that they and millions more like them might know that God is the God of the living, and not of the dead.

The Jews said, 'Behold how he loved him!' but can any Christian believe it was from love to Lazarus that Jesus wept? It was from love to God, and to Martha and Mary. He had not lost Lazarus; but Martha and Mary were astray from their father in heaven. 'Come, my brother; witness!' he cried; and Lazarus came forth, bound hand and foot. 'Loose him and let him go,' he said—a live truth walking about the world: he had never been dead, and was come forth; he had not been lost, and was restored! It was a strange door he came through, back to his own—a door seldom used, known only to one—but there he was! Oh, the hearts of Martha and Mary! Surely the Lord had some recompense for his trouble, beholding their joy!

Any Christian woman who has read thus far, I now beg to reflect on what I am going to put before her.

Lazarus had to die again, and thanked God, we may be sure, for the glad fact. Did his sisters, supposing them again left behind him in the world, make the same lamentations over him as the former time he went? If they did, if they fell again into that passion of grief, lamenting and moaning and refusing to be comforted, what would you say of them? I imagine something to this effect: 'It was most unworthy of them to be no better for such a favour shown them. It was to behave like the naughtiest of faithless children. Did they not know that he was not lost?—that he was with the Master, who had himself seemed lost for a few days, but came again? He was no more lost now than the time he went before! Could they not trust that he who brought him back once would take care they should have him for ever at last!' Would you not speak after some such fashion? Would you not remember that he who is the shepherd of the sheep will see that the sheep that love one another shall have their own again, in whatever different pastures they may feed for a time? Would it not be hard to persuade you that they ever did so behave? They must have felt that he was but 'gone for a minute . . . from this room into the next;' and that, however they might miss him, it would be a shame not to be patient when they knew there was nothing to fear. It was all right with him, and would soon be all right with them also!

'Yes,' I imagine you saying, 'that is just how they would feel!'

'Then,' I return, 'why are *you* so miserable? Or why is it but the cold frost of use and forgetting that makes you less miserable than you were a year ago?'

'Ah,' you answer, 'but I had no such miracle wrought for me! Ah, if I had such a miracle wrought for me, you should see then!'

'You mean that if your husband, your son, your father, your brother, your lover, had been taken from you once and given to you again, you would not, when the time came that he must go once more, dream of calling him a second time from the good heaven? You would not be cruel enough for that! You would not bemoan or lament! You would not make the heart of the Lord sad with your hopeless tears! Ah, how little you know yourself! Do you not see that, so far as truth and reason are concerned, you are now in precisely the position supposed—the position of those sisters after Lazarus was taken from them the second time? You know now all they knew then. They had no more of a revelation by the recall of Lazarus than you have. For you profess to believe the story, though you make that doubtful enough by your disregard of the very soul of it. Is it possible that, so far as you are concerned, Lazarus might as well not have risen? What difference is there between your position now and theirs? Lazarus was with God, and they knew he had gone, come back, and gone again. You know that he went, came, and went again. Your friend is gone as Lazarus went twice, and you behave as if you knew nothing of Lazarus. You make a lamentable ado, vexing Jesus that you will not be reasonable and trust his father!

When Martha and Mary behaved as you are doing, they had not had Lazarus raised; you have had Lazarus raised, yet you go on as they did then!

'You give too good reason to think that, if the same thing were done for you, you would say he was only in a cataleptic fit, and in truth was never raised from the dead. Or is there another way of understanding your behaviour: you do not believe that God is unchangeable, but think he acts one way one time and another way another time just from caprice? He might give back a brother to sisters who were favourites with him, but no such gift is to be counted upon? Why then, I ask, do you worship such a God?'

'But you know he does *not* do it! That was a mere exceptional case.'

'If it was, it is worthless indeed—as worthless as your behaviour would make it. But you are dull of heart, as were Martha and Mary. Do you not see that he is as continually restoring as taking away—that every bereavement is a restoration—that when you are weeping with void arms, others, who love as well as you, are clasping in ecstasy of reunion?'

'Alas, we know nothing about that!'

'If you have learned no more I must leave you, having no ground in you upon which my words may fall. You deceived me; you called yourself a Christian. You cannot have been doing the will of the Father, or you would not be as you are.'

'Ah, you little know my loss!'

'Indeed it is great! it seems to include God! If you knew what he knows about death you would clap your listless hands. But why should I seek in vain to comfort you? You must be made miserable, that you may wake from your sleep to know that you need God. If you do not find him, endless life with the living whom you bemoan would become and remain to you unendurable. The knowledge of your own heart will teach you this—not the knowledge you have, but the knowledge that is on its way to you through suffering. Then you will feel that existence itself is the prime of evils, without *the righteousness which is of God by faith.*'

RIGHTEOUSNESS.

—that I may win Christ, and be found in him, not having mine own righteousness, which is of the law, but that which is through the faith of Christ, the righteousness which is of God by faith.
Ep. to the Philippians iii. 8, 9.

WHAT does the apostle mean by the righteousness that is of God by faith? He means the same righteousness Christ had by his faith in God, the same righteousness God himself has.

In his second epistle to the Corinthians he says, 'He hath made him to be sin for us who knew no sin, that we might be made the righteousness of God in him;'—'He gave him to be treated like a sinner, killed and cast out of his own vineyard by his husbandmen, that we might in him be made righteous like God.' As the antithesis stands it is rhetorically correct. But if the former half means, 'he made him to be treated as if he were a sinner,' then the latter half should, in logical precision, mean, 'that we might be treated as if we were righteous.'

'That is just what Paul does mean,' insist not a few. 'He means that Jesus was treated by God as if he were a sinner, our sins being imputed to him, in order that we might be treated as if we were righteous, his righteousness being imputed to us.'

That is, that, by a sort of legal fiction, Jesus was treated as what he was not, in order that we might be treated as what we are not. This is the best device, according to the prevailing theology, that the God of truth, the God of mercy, whose glory is that he is just to men by forgiving their sins, could fall upon for saving his creatures!

I had thought that this most contemptible of false doctrines had nigh ceased to be presented, though I knew it must be long before it ceased to exercise baneful influence; but, to my astonishment, I came upon it lately in quite a modern commentary which I happened to look into in a friend's house. I say, to my astonishment, for the commentary was the work of one of the most liberal and lovely of Christians, a dignitary high in the church of England, a man whom I knew and love, and hope ere long to meet where there are no churches. In the comment that came under my eye, he refers to the doctrine of imputed righteousness as the possible explanation of a certain passage—refers to it as to a doctrine concerning whose truth was no question.

It seems to me that, seeing much duplicity exists in the body of Christ, every honest member of it should protest against any word tending to imply the existence of falsehood in the indwelling spirit of that body. I now protest against this so-called *doctrine*, counting it the rightful prey of the foolishest wind in the limbo of vanities, whither I would gladly do my best to send it. It is a mean, nauseous invention, false, and productive of falsehood. Say it is a figure, I answer it is not only a false figure but an embodiment of untruth; say it expresses a reality, and I say it teaches the worst of lies; say there is a shadow of truth in it, and I answer it may be so, but there is no truth touched in it that could not be taught infinitely better without it. It is the meagre misshapen offspring of the legalism of a poverty-stricken mechanical fancy, unlighted by a gleam of divine imagination. No one who knows his New Testament will dare to say that the figure is once used in it.

I have dealt already with the source of it.

They say first, God must punish the sinner, for justice requires it; then they say he does not punish the sinner, but punishes a perfectly righteous man instead, attributes his righteousness to the sinner, and so continues just. Was there ever such a confusion, such an inversion of right and wrong! Justice *could not* treat a righteous man as an unrighteous; neither, if justice required the punishment of sin, *could* justice let the sinner go unpunished. To lay the pain upon the righteous in the name of justice is simply monstrous. No wonder unbelief is rampant. Believe in Moloch if you will, but call him Moloch, not Justice. Be sure that the thing that God gives, the righteousness that is of God, is a real thing, and not a contemptible legalism. Pray God I have no righteousness imputed to me. Let me be regarded as the sinner I am; for nothing will serve my need but to be made a righteous man, one that will no more sin.

We have the word *imputed* just once in the New Testament. Whether the evil doctrine may have sprung from any possible misunderstanding of the passage where it occurs, I hardly care to inquire. The word as Paul uses it, and the whole of the thought whence his use of it springs, appeals to my sense of right and justice as much as the common use of it arouses my abhorrence. The apostle says that a certain thing was imputed to Abraham for righteousness; or, as the revised version has it, 'reckoned unto him:' what was it that was thus imputed to Abraham? The righteousness of another? God forbid! It was his own faith. The faith of Abraham is reckoned to him for righteousness. To impute the righteousness of one to another, is simply to act a falsehood; to call the faith of a man his righteousness is simply to speak the truth. Was it not righteous in Abraham to obey God? The Jews placed righteousness in keeping all the particulars of the law of Moses: Paul says faith in God was counted righteousness before Moses was born. You may answer, Abraham was unjust in many things, and by no means a righteous man. True; he was not a righteous man in any complete sense; his righteousness would never have satisfied Paul; neither, you may be sure, did it satisfy Abraham; but his faith was nevertheless righteousness, and if it had not been counted to him for righteousness, there would have been falsehood somewhere, for such faith as

Abraham's *is righteousness.* It was no mere intellectual recognition of the existence of a God, which is consistent with the deepest atheism; it was that faith which is one with action: 'He went out, not knowing whither he went.' The very act of believing in God after such fashion that, when the time of action comes, the man will obey God, is the highest act, the deepest, loftiest righteousness of which man is capable, is at the root of all other righteousness, and the spirit of it will work till the man is perfect. If you define righteousness in the common-sense, that is, in the divine fashion—for religion is nothing if it be not the deepest common-sense—as a giving to everyone his due, then certainly the first due is to him who makes us capable of owing, that is, makes us responsible creatures. You may say this is not one's first feeling of duty. True; but the first in reality is seldom the first perceived. The first duty is too high and too deep to come first into consciousness. If any one were born perfect, which I count an eternal impossibility, then the highest duty would come first into the consciousness. As we are born, it is the doing of, or at least the honest trying to do many another duty, that will at length lead a man to see that his duty to God is the first and deepest and highest of all, including and requiring the performance of all other duties whatever. A man might live a thousand years in neglect of duty, and never come to see that any obligation was upon him to put faith in God and do what he told him—never have a glimpse of the fact that he owed him something. I will allow that if God were what he thinks him he would indeed owe him little ; but he thinks him such in consequence of not doing what he knows he ought to do. He has not come to the light. He has deadened, dulled, hardened his nature. He has not been a man without guile, has not been true and fair.

But while faith in God is the first duty, and may therefore well be called righteousness in the man in whom it is operative, even though it be imperfect, there is more reason than this why it should be counted to a man for righteousness. It is the one spiritual act which brings the man into contact with the original creative power, able to help him in every endeavour after righteousness, and ensure his progress to perfection. The man who exercises it may therefore also well be called a righteous man, however far from complete in righteousness. We may call a woman beautiful who is not perfect in beauty ; in the Bible men are constantly recognized as righteous men who are far from perfectly righteous. The Bible never deals with impossibilities, never demands of any man at any given moment a righteousness of which at that moment he is incapable ; neither does it lay upon any man any other law than that of perfect righteousness. It demands of him righteousness ; when he yields that righteousness of which he is capable, content for the moment, it goes on to demand more : the common-sense of the Bible is lovely.

To the man who has no faith in God, faith in God cannot look like righteousness ; neither can he know that it is creative of all other righteousness toward equal and inferior lives : he cannot know that it is not merely the beginning of righteousness, but the germ of life, the active potency whence life-righteousness grows. It is not like some single separate act of righteousness ; it is the action of the whole man, turning to good from evil —turning his back on all that is opposed to righteousness, and starting on a road on which he cannot stop, in which he must go on growing more and more righteous, discovering more and more what righteousness is, and more and more what is unrighteous in himself. In the one act of believing in God—that is, of giving himself to do what he tells him—he abjures evil, both what he knows and what he does not yet know in himself. A man may indeed have turned to obey God, and yet be capable of many an injustice to his neighbour which he has not yet discovered to be an injustice; but as he goes on obeying, he will go on discovering. Not only will he grow more and more determined to be just, but he will grow more and more sensitive to the idea of injustice—I do not mean in others, but in himself. A man who continues capable of a known injustice to his neighbour, cannot be believed to have turned to God. At all events, a man cannot be near God, so as to be learning what is just toward God, and not be near his neighbour, so as to be learning what is unfair to him; for his will, which is the man, lays hold of righteousness, chooses to be righteous. If a man is to be blamed for not choosing righteousness, for not turning to the light, for not coming out of the darkness, then the man who does choose and turn and come out, is to be justified in his deed, and declared to be righteous. He is not yet thoroughly righteous, but is growing in and toward righteousness. He needs creative God, and time for will and effort. Not yet quite righteous, he cannot yet act quite righteously, for only the man in whom the image of God is perfected can live perfectly. Born into the world without righteousness, he cannot see, he cannot know, he is not in touch with perfect righteousness, and it would be the deepest injustice to demand of him, with a penalty, at any given moment, more than he knows how to yield; but it is the highest love constantly to demand of him perfect righteousness as what he must attain to. With what life and possibility is in him, he must keep turning to righteousness and abjuring iniquity, ever aiming at the perfection of God. Such an obedient faith is most justly and fairly, being all that God himself can require of the man, called by God righteousness in the man. It would not be enough for the righteousness of God, or Jesus, or any perfected saint, because they are capable of perfect righteousness, and, knowing what is perfect righteousness, choose to be perfectly righteous; but, in virtue of the life and growth in it, it is enough at a given moment for the disciple of the Perfect. The righteousness of Abraham was not to compare with the righteousness of Paul. He did not fight with himself for righteousness, as did Paul—not because he was better than Paul and therefore did not need to fight, but because his idea of what was required of him was not within sight of that of Paul; yet was he righteous in the same way as Paul was righteous: he had begun to be righteous, and God called his righteousness righteousness, for faith is righteousness. His faith was an act recognizing God as his law, and that is not a partial act, but an all-embracing and all-determining action. A single righteous deed toward one's fellow could hardly be imputed to a man as righteousness. A man who is not trying after righteousness may yet do many a righteous act: they will not be forgotten to him, neither will they be imputed to him as righteousness. Abraham's action of obedient faith was righteousness none the less that his righteousness was far behind Paul's. Abraham started at the beginning of the long, slow, disappointing preparation of the Jewish people; Paul started at its close, with the story of Jesus behind him. Both believed, obeying God, and therefore both were righteous. They were righteous because they gave themselves up to God to make them righteous; and not to call such men righteous, not to impute their faith to them for righteousness, would be unjust. But God is utterly just, and nowise resembles a legal-minded Roman emperor, or a bad pope formulating the doctrine of vicarious sacrifice.

What, then, is the righteousness which is of God by faith? It is simply the thing that God wants every man to be, wrought out in him by constant obedient contact with God himself. It is not an attribute either of God or man, but a fact of character in God and in man. It is God's righteousness wrought out in us, so that as he is righteous we too are righteous. It does not consist in obeying this or that law; not even the keeping of every law, so that no hair's-breadth did we run counter to one of them, would be righteousness. To be righteous is to be such a heart, soul, mind, and will, as, without regard to law, would recoil with horror from the lightest possible breach of any law. It is to be so in love with what is fair and right as to make it impossible for a man to do anything that is less than absolutely righteous. It is not the love of righteousness in the abstract that makes anyone righteous, but such a love of fairplay toward everyone with whom we come into contact, that anything less than the fulfilling, with a clear joy, of our divine relation to him or her, is impossible. For the righteousness of God goes far beyond mere deeds, and requires of us love and helping mercy as our highest obligation and justice to our fellow men—those of them too who have done nothing for us, those even who have done us wrong. Our relations with others, God first and then our neighbour in order and degree, must one day become, as in true nature they are, the gladness of our being; and nothing then will ever appear good for us, that is not in harmony with those blessed relations. Every thought will not merely be just, but will be just because it is something more, because it is live and true. What heart in the kingdom of heaven would ever dream of constructing a metaphysical system of what we owed to God and why we owed it? The light of our life, our sole, eternal, and infinite joy, is simply God—God—God—nothing but God, and all his creatures in him. He is all and in all, and the children of the kingdom know it. He includes all things; not to be true to anything he has made is to be untrue to him. God is truth, is life; to be in God is to know him and need no law. Existence will be eternal Godness.

You would not like that way of it? There is, there can be, no other; but before you can judge of it, you must know at least a little of God as he is, not as you imagine him. I say *as you imagine him*, because it cannot be that any creature should know him as he is and not desire him. In proportion as we know him we must desire him, until at length we live in and for him with all our conscious heart. That is why the Jews did not like the Lord: he cared so simply for his father's will, and not for anything they called his will.

The righteousness which is of God by faith in the source, the prime of that righteousness, is then just the same kind of thing as God's righteousness, differing only as the created differs from the creating. The righteousness of him who does the will of his father in heaven, is the righteousness of Jesus Christ, is God's own righteousness. The righteousness which is of God by faith in God, is God's righteousness. The man who has this righteousness, thinks about things as God thinks about them, loves the things that God loves, cares for nothing that God does not care about. Even while this righteousness is being born in him, the man will say to himself, 'Why should I be troubled about this thing or that? Does God care about it? No. Then why should I care? I must not care. I will not care!' If he does not know whether God cares about it or not, he will say, 'If God cares I should have my desire, he will give it me; if he does not care I should have it, neither will I care. In the meantime I will do my work.' The man with God's righteousness does not love a thing merely because it is right, but loves the very rightness in it. He not only loves a thought, but he loves the man in his thinking that thought; he loves the thought alive in the man. He does not take his joy from himself. He feels joy in himself, but it comes to him from others, not from himself—from God first, and from somebody, anybody, everybody next. He would rather, in the fulness of his content, pass out of being, rather himself cease to exist, than that another should. He could do without knowing himself, but he could not know himself and spare one of the brothers or sisters God had given him. The man who really knows God, is, and always will be, content with what God, who is the very self of his self, shall choose for him; he is entirely God's, and not at all his own. His consciousness of himself is the reflex from those about him, not the result of his own turning in of his regard upon himself. It is not the contemplation of what God has made him, it is the being what God has made him, and the contemplation of what God himself is, and what he has made his fellows, that gives him his joy. He wants nothing, and feels that he has all things, for he is in the bosom of his father, and the thoughts of his father come to him. He knows that if he needs anything, it is his before he asks it; for his father has willed him, in the might and truth of his fatherhood, to be one with himself.

This then, or something like this, for words are poor to tell the best things, is the righteousness which is of God by faith—so far from being a thing built on the rubbish heap of legal fiction called vicarious sacrifice, or its shadow called imputed righteousness, that only the child with the child-heart, so far ahead of and so different from the wise and prudent, can understand it. The wise and prudent interprets God by himself, and does not understand him; the child interprets

God by himself, and does understand him. The wise and prudent must make a system and arrange things to his mind before he can say, *I believe.* The child sees, believes, obeys—and knows he must be perfect as his father in heaven is perfect. If an angel, seeming to come from heaven, told him that God had let him off, that he did not require so much of him as that, but would be content with less; that he could not indeed allow him to be wicked, but would pass by a great deal, modifying his demands because it was so hard for him to be quite good, and he loved him so dearly, the child of God would at once recognize, woven with the angel's starry brilliancy, the flicker of the flames of hell, and would say to the shining one, 'Get thee behind me, Satan.' Nor would there be the slightest wonder or merit in his doing so, for at the words of the deceiver, if but for briefest moment imagined true, the shadow of a rising hell would gloom over the face of creation; hope would vanish; the eternal would be as the carcase of a dead man; the glory would die out of the face of God—until the groan of a thunderous *no* burst from the caverns of the universe, and the truth, flashing on his child's soul from the heart of the Eternal,

Immortal, Invisible, withered up the lie of the messenger of darkness.

'But how can God bring this about in me?'

Let him do it, and perhaps you will know; if you never know, yet there it will be. Help him to do it, or he cannot do it. He originates the possibility of your being his son, his daughter; he makes you able to will it, but you must will it. If he is not doing it in you—that is, if you have as yet prevented him from beginning, why should I tell you, even if I knew the process, how he would do what you will not let him do? Why should you know? What claim have you to know? But indeed how should you be able to know? For it must deal with deeper and higher things than you *can* know anything of till the work is at least begun. Perhaps if you approved of the plans of the glad creator, you would allow him to make of you something divine! To teach your intellect what has to be learned by your whole being, what cannot be understood without the whole being, what it would do you no good to understand save you understood it in your whole being—if this be the province of any man, it is not mine. Let the dead bury their dead, and the dead teach their dead; for me, I will try to wake them. To those who are awake, I cry, 'For the sake of your father and the first-born among many brethren to whom we belong, for the sake of those he has given us to love the most dearly, let patience have her perfect work. Statue under the chisel of the sculptor, stand steady to the blows of his mallet. Clay on the wheel, let the fingers of the divine potter model you at their will. Obey the Father's lightest word; hear the Brother who knows you, and died for you; beat down your sin, and trample it to death.

Brother, when thou sittest at home in thy house, which is the temple of the Lord, open all thy windows to breathe the air of his approach; set the watcher on thy turret, that he may listen out into the dark for the sound of his coming, and thy hand be on the latch to open the door at his first knock. Shouldst thou open the door and not see him, do not say he did not knock, but understand that he is there, and wants thee to go out to him. It may be he has something for thee to do for him. Go and do it, and perhaps thou wilt return with a new prayer, to find a new window in thy soul.

Never wait for fitter time or place to talk to him. To wait till thou go to church, or to thy closet, is to make *him* wait. He will listen as thou walkest in the lane or the crowded street, on the common or in the place of shining concourse.

Remember, if indeed thou art able to know it, that not in any church is the service done that he requires. He will say to no man, 'You never went to church: depart from me; I do not know you;' but, 'Inasmuch as you never helped one of my father's children, you have done nothing for me.' Church or chapel is *not* the place for divine service. It is a place of prayer, a place of praise, a place to feed upon good things, a place to learn of God, as what place is not? It is a place to look in the eyes of your neighbour, and love God along with him. But the world in which you move, the place of your living and loving and labour, not the church you go to on your holiday, is the place of divine service. Serve your neighbour, and you serve him.

Do not heed much if men mock you and speak lies of you, or in goodwill defend you unworthily. Heed not much if even the righteous turn their backs upon you. Only take heed that you turn not from them. Take courage in the fact that *there is nothing covered, that shall not be revealed; and hid, that shall not be known.*

THE FINAL UNMASKING.

>For there is nothing covered, that shall not be revealed; and hid, that shall not be known.—*Matthew* x. 26; *Luke* xii. 2.

GOD is not a God that hides, but a God that reveals. His whole work in relation to the creatures he has made—and where else can lie his work?—is revelation—the giving them truth, the showing of himself to them, that they may know him, and come nearer and nearer to him, and so he have his children more and more of companions to him. That we are in the dark about anything is never because he hides it, but because we are not yet such that he is able to reveal that thing to us.

That God could not do the thing at once which he takes time to do, we may surely say without irreverence. His will cannot finally be thwarted; where it is thwarted for a time, the very thwarting subserves the working out of a higher part of his will. He gave man the power to thwart his will, that, by means of that same power, he might come at last to do his will in a higher kind and way than would otherwise have been possible to him. God sacrifices his will to man that man may become such as himself, and give all to the truth; he makes man able to do wrong, that he may choose and love righteousness.

The fact that all things are slowly coming into the light of the knowledge of men—so far as this may be possible to the created—is used in three different ways by the Lord, as reported by his evangelists. In one case, with which we will not now occupy ourselves—*Mark* iv. 22; *Luke* viii. 16—he uses it to enforce the duty of those who have received light to let it shine: they must do their part to bring all things out. In *Luke* xii. 2, is recorded how he brought it to bear on hypocrisy, showing its uselessness; and, in the case recorded in *Matthew* x. 25, he uses the fact to enforce fearlessness as to the misinterpretation of our words and actions.

In whatever mode the Lord may intend that it shall be wrought out, he gives us to understand, as an unalterable principle in the government of the universe, that all such things as the unrighteous desire to conceal, and such things as it is a pain to the righteous to have concealed, shall come out into the light.

'Beware of hypocrisy,' the Lord says, 'for there is nothing covered, that shall not be revealed, neither hid, that shall not be known.' What is hypocrisy? The desire to look better than you are; the hiding of things you do, because you would not be supposed to do them, because you would be ashamed to have them known where you are known. The doing of them is foul; the hiding of them, in order to appear better than you are, is fouler still. The man who does not live in his own consciousness as in the open heavens, is a hypocrite—and for most of us the question is, are we growing less or more of such hypocrites? Are we ashamed of not having been open and clear? Are we fighting the evil thing which is our temptation to hypocrisy? The Lord has not a thought in him to be ashamed of before God and his universe, and he will not be content until he has us in the same liberty. For our encouragement to fight on, he tells us that those that hunger and thirst after righteousness shall be filled, that they shall become as righteous as the spirit of the Father and the Son in them can make them desire.

The Lord says also, 'If they have called the master of the house Beelzebub, how much more shall they call them of his household! Fear them not therefore: for there is nothing covered, that shall not be revealed; and hid, that shall not be known.' To a man who loves righteousness and his fellow men, it must always be painful to be misunderstood; and misunderstanding is specially inevitable where he acts upon principles beyond the recognition of those around him, who, being but half-hearted Christians, count themselves the law-givers of righteousness, and charge him with the very things it is the aim of his life to destroy. The Lord himself was accused of being a drunkard and a keeper of bad company—and perhaps would in the present day be so regarded by not a few calling themselves by his name, and teaching temperance and virtue. He lived upon a higher spiritual platform than they understand, acted from a height of the virtues they would inculcate, loftier than their eyes can scale. His Himalays are not visible from their sand-heaps. The Lord bore with their evil tongues, and was neither dismayed nor troubled;

but from this experience of his own, comforts those who, being his messengers, must fare as he. 'If they have called the master of the house Beelzebub, how much more shall they call them of his household!'—'If they insult a man, how much more will they not insult his servants!' While men count themselves Christians on any other ground than that they are slaves of Jesus Christ, the children of God, and free from themselves, so long will they use the servants of the Master despitefully. 'Do not hesitate,' says the Lord, 'to speak the truth that is in you; never mind what they call you; proclaim from the housetop; fear nobody.'

He spoke the words to the men to whom he looked first to spread the news of the kingdom of heaven; but they apply to all who obey him. Few who have endeavoured to do their duty, have not been annoyed, disappointed, enraged perhaps, by the antagonism, misunderstanding, and false representation to which they have been subjected therein—issuing mainly from those and the friends of those who have benefited by their efforts to be neighbours to all. The tales of heartlessness and ingratitude one must come across, compel one to see more and more clearly that humanity, without willed effort after righteousness, is mean enough to sink to any depth of disgrace. The judgments also of imagined superiority are hard to bear. The rich man who will screw his workmen to the lowest penny, will read his poor relation a solemn lecture on extravagance, because of some humblest little act of generosity! He takes the end of the beam sticking out of his eye to pick the mote from the eye of his brother withal! If, in the endeavour to lead a truer life, a man merely lives otherwise than his neighbours, strange motives will be invented to account for it. To the honest soul it is a comfort to believe that the truth will one day be known, that it will cease to be supposed that he was and did as dull heads and hearts reported of him. Still more satisfactory will be the unveiling where a man is misunderstood by those who ought to know him better—who, not even understanding the point at issue, take it for granted he is about to do the wrong thing, while he is crying for courage to heed neither himself nor his friends, but only the Lord. How many hear and accept the words, 'Be not conformed to this world,' without once perceiving that what they call Society and bow to as supreme, is the World and nothing else, or that those who mind what people think, and what people will say, are conformed to—that is, take the shape of—the world. The true man feels he has nothing to do with Society as judge or lawgiver: he is under the law of Jesus Christ, and it sets him free from the law of the World. Let a man do right, nor trouble himself about worthless opinion; the less he heeds tongues, the less difficult will he find it to love men. Let him comfort himself with the thought that the truth must out. He will not have to pass through eternity with the brand of ignorant or malicious judgment upon him. He shall find his peers and be judged of them.

But, thou who lookest for the justification of the light, art thou verily prepared for thyself to encounter such exposure as the general unveiling of things must bring? Art thou willing for the truth whatever it be? I nowise mean to ask, Have you a conscience so void of offence, have you a heart so pure and clean, that you fear no fullest exposure of what is in you to the gaze of men and angels? —as to God, he knows it all now! What I mean to ask is, Do you so love the truth and the right, that you welcome, or at least submit willingly to the idea of an exposure of what in you is yet unknown to yourself—an exposure that may redound to the glory of the truth by making you ashamed and humble? It may be, for instance, that you were wrong in regard to those, for the righting of whose wrongs to you, the great judgment of God is now by you waited for with desire: will you welcome any discovery, even if it work for the excuse of others, that will make you more true, by revealing what in you was false? Are you willing to be made glad that you were wrong when you thought others were wrong? If you can with such submission face the revelation of things hid, then you are of the truth, and need not be afraid; for, whatever comes, it will and can only make you more true and humble and pure.

Does the Lord mean that everything a man has ever done or thought must be laid bare to the universe?

So far, I think, as is necessary to the understanding of the man by those who have known, or are concerned to know him. For the time to come, and for those who are yet to know him, the man will henceforth, if he is a true man, be transparent to all that are capable of reading him. A man may not then, any more than now, be intelligible to those beneath him, but all things will be working toward revelation, nothing toward concealment or misunderstanding. Who in the kingdom will desire concealment, or be willing to misunderstand? Concealment is darkness; misunderstanding is a fog. A man will hold the door open for anyone to walk into his house, for it is a temple of the living God—with some things worth looking at, and nothing to hide. The glory of the true world is, that there is nothing in it that needs to be covered, while ever and ever there will be things uncovered. Every man's light will shine for the good and glory of his neighbour.

'Will all my weaknesses, all my evil habits, all my pettinesses, all the wrong thoughts which I cannot help—will all be set out before the universe?'

Yes, if they so prevail as to constitute your character—that is, if they are you. But if you have come out of the darkness, if you are fighting it, if you are honestly trying to walk in the light, you may hope in God your father that what he has cured, what he is curing, what he has forgiven, will be heard of no more, not now being a constituent part of you. Or if indeed some of your evil things must yet be seen, the truth of them will be seen—that they are things you are at strife with, not things you are cherishing and brooding over. God will be fair to you—so fair!—fair with the fairness of a father loving his own—who will have you clean, who will neither spare you any needful shame, nor leave you exposed to any that is not needful. The thing we have risen above, is dead and forgotten, or if remembered, there is God to comfort us. 'If any man sin, we have a comforter with the Father.' We may trust God with our past as heartily as with our future. It will not hurt us so long as we do not try to hide things, so long as we are ready to bow our heads in hearty shame where it is fit we should be ashamed. For to be ashamed is a holy and blessed thing. Shame is a thing to shame only those who want to appear, not those who want to be. Shame is to shame those who want to pass their examination, not those who would get into the heart of things. In the name of God let us henceforth have nothing to be ashamed of, and be ready to meet any shame on its way to meet us. For to be humbly ashamed is to be plunged in the cleansing bath of the truth.

As to the revelation of the ways of God, I need

not speak; he has been always, from the first, revealing them to his prophet, to his child, and will go on doing so for ever. But let me say a word about another kind of revelation—that of their own evil to the evil.

The only terrible, or at least the supremely terrible revelation is that of a man to himself. What a horror will it not be to a vile man—more than all to a man whose pleasure has been enhanced by the suffering of others—a man that knew himself such as men of ordinary morals would turn from with disgust, but who has hitherto had no insight into what he is—what a horror will it not be to him when his eyes are opened to see himself as the pure see him, as God sees him! Imagine such a man waking all at once, not only to see the eyes of the universe fixed upon him with loathing astonishment, but to see himself at the same moment as those eyes see him! What a waking!—into the full blaze of fact and consciousness, of truth and violation!

To know my deed, 'twere best not know myself!

Or think what it must be for a man counting himself religious, orthodox, exemplary, to perceive suddenly that there was no religion in him, only love of self; no love of the right, only a great love of being in the right! What a discovery—that he was simply a hypocrite—one who loved to *appear*, and *was* not! The rich seem to be those among whom will occur hereafter the sharpest reverses, if I understand aright the parable of the rich man and Lazarus. Who has not known the insolence of their meanness toward the poor, all the time counting themselves of the very elect! What riches and fancied religion, with the self-sufficiency they generate between them, can make man or woman capable of, is appalling. Mammon, the most contemptible of deities, is the most worshipped, both outside and in the house of God : to many of the religious rich in that day, the great damning revelation will be their behaviour to the poor to whom they thought themselves very kind. 'He flattereth himself in his own eyes until his iniquity is found to be hateful.' A man may loathe a thing in the abstract for years, and find at last that all the time he has been, in his own person, guilty of it. To carry a thing under our cloak caressingly, hides from us its identity with something that stands before us on the public pillory. Many a man might read this and assent to it, who cages in his own bosom a carrion-bird that he never knows for what it is, because there are points of difference in its plumage from that of the bird he calls by an ugly name.

Of all who will one day stand in dismay and sickness of heart, with the consciousness that their very existence is a shame, those will fare the worst who have been consciously false to their fellows; who, pretending friendship, have used their neighbour to their own ends; and especially those who, pretending friendship, have divided friends. To such Dante has given the lowest hell. If there be one thing God hates, it must be treachery. Do not imagine Judas the only man of whom the Lord would say, 'Better were it for that man if he had never been born!' Did the Lord speak out of personal indignation, or did he utter a spiritual fact, a live principle? Did he speak in anger at the treachery of his apostle to himself, or in pity for the man that had better not have been born? Did the word spring from his knowledge of some fearful punishment awaiting Judas, or from his sense of the horror it was to be such a man? Beyond all things pitiful is it that a man should carry about with him the consciousness of being such a person—should know himself and not another that false one! 'O God,' we think, 'how terrible if it were I!' Just so terrible is it that it should be Judas! And have I not done things with the same germ in them, a germ which, brought to its evil perfection, would have shown itself the canker-worm, treachery? Except I love my neighbour as myself, I may one day betray him! Let us therefore be compassionate and humble, and hope for every man.

A man may sink by such slow degrees that, long after he is a devil, he may go on being a good churchman or a good dissenter, and thinking himself a good Christian. Continuously repeated sin against the poorest consciousness of evil must have a dread rousing. There are men who never wake to know how wicked they are, till, lo, the gaze of the multitude is upon them!—the multitude staring with self-righteous eyes, doing like things themselves, but not yet found out; sinning after another pattern, therefore the hardest judges, thinking by condemnation to escape judgment. But there is nothing covered that shall not be revealed.

What if the only thing to wake the treacherous, money-loving thief, Judas, to a knowledge of himself, was to let the thing go on to the end, and his kiss betray the Master? Judas did not hate the Master when he kissed him, but not being a true man, his very love betrayed him.

The good man, conscious of his own evil, and desiring no refuge but the purifying light, will chiefly rejoice that the exposure of evil makes for the victory of the truth, the kingdom of God and his Christ. He sees in the unmasking of the hypocrite, in the unveiling of the covered, in the exposure of the hidden, God's interference, for him and all the race, between them and the lie.

The only triumph the truth can ever have is its recognition by the heart of the liar. Its victory is in the man who, not content with saying, 'I was blind and now I see,' cries out, 'Lord God, just and true, let me perish, but endure thou! Let me live because thou livest, because thou savest me from the death in myself, the untruth I have nourished in me, and even called righteousness! Hallowed be thy name, for thou only art true; thou only lovest; thou only art holy, for thou only art humble! Thou only art unselfish; thou only hast never sought thine own, but the things of thy children! Yea, O father, be thou true, and every man a liar!'

There is no satisfaction of revenge possible to the injured. The severest punishment that can be inflicted upon the wrong-doer is simply to let him know what he is; for his nature is of God, and the deepest in him is the divine. Neither can any other punishment than the sinner's being made to see the enormity of his injury, give satisfaction to the injured. While the wronger will admit no wrong, while he mocks at the idea of amends, or while, admitting the wrong, he rejoices in having done it, no suffering could satisfy revenge, far less justice. Both would continually know themselves foiled. Therefore, while a satisfied justice is an unavoidable eternal event, a satisfied revenge is an eternal impossibility. For the moment that the sole adequate punishment, a vision of himself, begins to take true effect upon the sinner, that moment the sinner has begun to grow a righteous man, and the brother human whom he has offended has no choice, has nothing left him but to take the offender to his bosom—the more tenderly that his brother is a repentant brother, that he was dead and is alive again, that he was lost and is found. Behold the meeting of the divine extremes —the extreme of punishment, the embrace of heaven! They run together; 'the wheel is come full circle.' For, I venture to think, there can be no such agony for created soul, as to see itself vile —vile by its own action and choice. Also I venture to think there can be no delight for created soul—short, that is, of being one with the Father— so deep as that of seeing the heaven of forgiveness open, and disclose the shining stair that leads to its own natural home, where the eternal Father has been all the time awaiting this return of his child.

So, friends, however indignant we may be, however intensely and however justly we may feel our wrongs, there is no revenge possible for us in the universe of the Father. I may say to myself with heartiest vengeance, 'I should just like to let that man see what a wretch he is—what all honest men at this moment think of him!' but, the moment come, the man will loathe himself tenfold more than any other man could, and that moment my heart will bury his sin. Its own ocean of pity will rush from the divine depths of its God-origin to overwhelm it. Let us try to forethink, to antedate our forgiveness. Dares any man suppose that Jesus would have him hate the traitor through whom he came to the cross? Has he been pleased through all these ages with the manner in which those calling themselves by his name have treated, and are still treating his nation? We have not yet sounded the depths of forgiveness that are and will be required of such as would be his disciples!

Our friends will know us then: for their joy, will it be, or their sorrow? Will their hearts sink within them when they look on the real likeness of us? Or will they rejoice to find that we were not so much to be blamed as they thought, in this thing or that which gave them trouble?

Let us remember, however, that not evil only will be unveiled; that many a masking misconception will uncover a face radiant with the loveliness of the truth. And whatever disappointments may fall, there is consolation for every true heart in the one sufficing joy—that it stands on the border of the kingdom, about to enter into ever fuller, ever-growing possession *of the inheritance of the saints in light.*

THE INHERITANCE.

Giving thanks unto the Father, which hath made us meet to be partakers of the inheritance of the saints in light.—*Ep. to the Colossians* i. 12.

To have a share in any earthly inheritance, is to diminish the share of the other inheritors. In the inheritance of the saints, that which each has, goes to increase the possession of the rest. Hear what Dante puts in the mouth of his guide, as they pass through Purgatory :—

> Perchè s' appuntano i vostri desiri
> Dove per compagnia parte si scema,
> Invidia muove il mantaco a' sospiri.
> Ma se l' amor della spera suprema
> Torcesse 'n suso 'l desiderio vostro,
> Non vi sarebbe al petto quella tema ;
> Che per quanto si dice più lì nostro,
> Tanto possiede più di ben ciascuno,
> E più di caritade arde in quel chiostro.

> Because you point and fix your longing eyes
> On things where sharing lessens every share,

> The human bellows heave with envious sighs.
> But if the loftiest love that dwelleth there
> > Up to the heaven of heavens your longing turn,
> > Then from your heart will pass this fearing care:
> The oftener there the word *our* they discern,
> > The more of good doth everyone possess,
> > The more of love doth in that cloister burn.

Dante desires to know how it can be that a distributed good should make the receivers the richer the more of them there are; and Virgil answers—

> > Perocchè tu rificchi
> > > La mente pure alle cose terrene,
> > > Di vera luce tenebre dispicchi.
> > Quello 'nfinito ed ineffabil bene,
> > > Che lassù è, così corre ad amore,
> > > Com' a lucido corpo raggio viene.
> > Tanto si dà, quanto truova d' ardore:
> > > Sì che quantunque carità si stende,
> > > Cresce sovr' essa l' eterno valore.
> > E quanta gente più lassù s' intende,
> > > Più v' è da bene amare, e più vi s' ama,
> > > E come specchio, l' uno all' altro rende.

> > Because thy mind doth stick
> > To earthly things, and on them only brood,
> > From the true light thou dost but darkness pick.
> > That same ineffable and infinite Good,

> Which dwells up there, to Love doth run as fleet
> As sunrays to bright things, for sisterhood.
> It gives itself proportionate to the heat :
> So that, wherever Love doth spread its reign,
> The growing wealth of God makes that its seat.
> And the more people that up thither strain,
> The more there are to love, the more they love,
> And like a mirror each doth give and gain.

In this inheritance then a man may desire and endeavour to obtain his share without selfish prejudice to others; nay, to fail of our share in it, would be to deprive others of a portion of theirs. Let us look a little nearer, and see in what the inheritance of the saints consists.

It might perhaps be to commit some small logical violence on the terms of the passage to say that 'the inheritance of the saints in light' *must* mean purely and only 'the possession of light which is the inheritance of the saints.' At the same time the phrase is literally 'the inheritance of the saints *in the light*;' and this perhaps makes it the more likely that, as I take it, Paul had in his mind the light as itself the inheritance of the saints—that he held the very substance of the inheritance to be the light. And if we remember that God is light; also that the highest prayer of the Lord for his friends was that they might be one in him and his father; and recall what the apostle said to the Ephesians, that 'in him we live and move and have our being,' we may be prepared to agree that, although he may not mean to include all possible phases of the inheritance of the saints in the one word *light*, as I think he does, yet the idea is perfectly consistent with his teaching. For the one only thing to make existence a good, the one thing to make it worth having, is just that there should be no film of separation between our life and the life of which ours is an outcome; that we should not only *know* that God is our life, but be aware, in some grand consciousness beyond anything imagination can present to us, of the presence of the making God, in the very process of continuing us the live things he has made us. This is only another way of saying that the very inheritance upon which, as the twice-born sons of our father, we have a claim—which claim his sole desire for us is that we should, so to say, enforce—that this inheritance is simply the light, God himself, the Light. If you think of ten thousand things that are good and worth having, what is it that makes them good or worth having but the God in them? That the loveliness of the world has its origin in the making will of God, would not content me; I say, the very loveliness of it is the loveliness of God, for its loveliness is his own lovely thought, and must be a revelation of that which dwells and moves in himself. Nor is this all: my interest in its loveliness would vanish, I should feel that the soul was out of it, if you could persuade me that God had ceased to care for the daisy, and now cared for something else instead. The faces of some flowers lead me back to the heart of God; and, as his child, I hope I feel, in my lowly degree, what he felt when, brooding over them, he said, 'They are good;' that is, 'They are what I mean.'

The thing I am reasoning toward is this: that, if everything were thus seen in its derivation from God, then the inheritance of the saints, whatever the form of their possession, would be seen to be light. All things are God's, not as being in his power—that of course—but as coming from him. The darkness itself becomes light around him when we think that verily he hath created the darkness, for there could have been no darkness but for the light. Without God there would not even have been nothing; there would not have existed the idea of nothing, any more than any reality of nothing, but that he exists and called *something* into being.

Nothingness owes its very name and nature to the being and reality of God. There is no word to represent that which is not God, no word for the *where* without God in it; for it is not, could not be. So I think we may say that the inheritance of the saints is the share each has in the Light.

But how can any share exist where all is open?

The true share, in the heavenly kingdom throughout, is not what you have to keep, but what you have to give away. The thing that is mine is the thing I have with the power to give it. The thing I have *no* power to give a share in, is nowise mine; the thing I cannot share with everyone, cannot be essentially my own. The cry of the thousand splendours which Dante, in the fifth canto of the 'Paradiso,' tells us he saw gliding toward them in the planet Mercury, was—

> Ecco chi crescerà li nostri amori!
>
> Lo, here comes one who will increase our loves!

All the light is ours. God is all ours. Even that in God which we cannot understand is ours. If there were anything in God that was not ours, then God would not be one God. I do not say we must, or can ever know all in God; not throughout eternity shall we ever comprehend God, but he is our father, and must think of us with every part of him—so to speak in our poor speech; he must know us, and that in himself which we cannot know, with the same thought, for he is one. We and that which we do not or cannot know, come together in his thought. And this helps us to see how, claiming all things, we have yet shares. For the infinitude of God can only begin and only go on to be revealed, through his infinitely differing creatures—all capable of wondering at, admiring, and loving each other, and so bound all in one in him, each to the others revealing him. For every human being is like a facet cut in the great diamond to which I may dare liken the father of him who likens his kingdom to a pearl. Every man, woman, child—for the incomplete also is his, and in its very incompleteness reveals him as a progressive worker in his creation—is a revealer of God. I have my message of my great Lord, you have yours. Your dog, your horse tells you about him who cares for all his creatures. None of them came from his *hands*. Perhaps the precious things of the earth, the coal and the diamonds, the iron and clay and gold, may be said to have come from his hands; but the live things come from his heart—from near the same region whence ourselves we came. How much my horse may, in his own fashion—that is, God's equine way—know of him, I cannot tell, because he cannot tell. Also, we do not know what the horses know, because they are horses, and we are at best, in relation to them, only horsemen. The ways of God go down into microscopic depths, as well as up into telescopic heights —and with more marvel, for there lie the beginnings of life: the immensities of stars and worlds all exist for the sake of less things than they. So with mind; the ways of God go into the depths yet unrevealed to us; he knows his horses and dogs as we cannot know them, because we are not yet pure sons of God. When through our sonship, as Paul teaches, the redemption of these lower brothers and sisters shall have come, then we shall understand each other better But now the lord of life has to look on at the wilful torture of multitudes of his creatures. It must be that offences come, but woe unto that man by whom they come! The Lord may seem not to heed, but he sees and knows.

I say, then, that every one of us is something that the other is not, and therefore knows something—it may be without knowing that he knows it—which no one else knows; and that it is every one's business, as one of the kingdom of light, and inheritor in it all, to give his portion to the rest; for we are one family, with God at the head and the heart of it, and Jesus Christ, our elder brother, teaching us of the Father, whom he only knows.

We may say, then, that whatever is the source of joy or love, whatever is pure and strong, whatever wakes aspiration, whatever lifts us out of selfishness, whatever is beautiful or admirable—in a word, whatever is of the light—must make a part, however small it may then prove to be in its proportion, of the inheritance of the saints in the light; for, as in the epistle of James, 'Every good gift, and every perfect gift is from above, and cometh down from the Father of lights, with whom is no variableness, neither shadow of turning.'

Children fear heaven, because of the dismal notions the unchildlike give them of it, who, without imagination, receive unquestioning what others, as void of imagination as themselves, represent concerning it. I do not see that one should care to present an agreeable picture of it; for, suppose I could persuade a man that heaven was the perfection of all he could desire around him, what would the man or the truth gain by it? If he knows the Lord, he will not trouble himself about heaven; if he does not know him, he will not be drawn to *him* by it. I would not care to persuade the feeble Christian that heaven was a place worth going to; I would rather persuade him that no spot in space, no hour in eternity is worth anything to one who remains such as he is. But would that none presumed to teach the little ones what they know nothing of themselves! What have not children suffered from strong endeavour to desire the things they could not love! Well do I remember the pain of the prospect—no, the trouble at not being pleased with the prospect—of being made a pillar in the house of God, and going no more out! Those words were not spoken to the little ones. Yet are they, literally taken, a blessed promise compared with the notion of a continuous church-going! Perhaps no one teaches such a thing; but somehow the children get the dreary fancy: there are ways of involuntary teaching more potent than words. What boy, however fain to be a disciple of Christ and a child of God, would prefer a sermon to his glorious kite, that divinest of toys, with God himself for his playmate, in the blue wind that tossed it hither and thither in the golden void! He might be ready to part with kite and wind and sun, and go down to the grave for his brothers—but surely not that they might be admitted to an everlasting prayer-meeting! For my own part, I rejoice to think that there will be neither church nor chapel in the high countries; yea, that there will be nothing there called religion, and no law but the perfect law of liberty. For how should there be law or religion where every throb of the heart says *God*! where every song-throat is eager with thanksgiving! where such a tumult of glad waters is for ever bursting from beneath the throne of God, the tears of the gladness of the universe! Religion? Where will be the room for it, when the essence of every thought must be God? Law? What room will there be for law, when everything upon which law could lay a *shalt not* will be too loathsome to think of?

What room for honesty, where love fills full the law to overflowing—where a man would rather drop sheer into the abyss, than wrong his neighbour one hair's-breadth?

Heaven will be continuous touch with God. The very sense of being will in itself be bliss. For the sense of true life, there must be actual, conscious contact with the source of the life; therefore mere life—in itself, in its very essence good—good as the life of God which is our life—must be such bliss as, I think, will need the mitigation of the loftiest joys of communion with our blessed fellows; the mitigation of art in every shape, and of all combinations of arts; the mitigation of countless services to the incomplete, and hard toil for those who do not yet know their neighbour or their Father. The bliss of pure being will, I say, need these mitigations to render the intensity of it endurable by heart and brain.

To those who care only for things, and not for the souls of them, for the truth, the reality of them, the prospect of inheriting light can have nothing attractive, and for their comfort—how false a comfort!—they may rest assured there is no danger of their being required to take up their inheritance at present. Perhaps they will be left to go on sucking *things* dry, constantly missing the loveliness of them, until they come at last to loathe the lovely husks, turned to ugliness in their false imaginations. Loving but the body of Truth, even here they come to call it a lie, and break out in maudlin moaning over the illusions of life. The soul of Truth they have lost, because they never loved her. What may they not have to pass through, what purifying fires, before they can even behold her!

The notions of Christians, so called, concerning the state into which they suppose their friends to have entered, and which they speak of as a place of blessedness, are yet such as to justify the bitterness of their lamentation over them, and the heathenish doubt whether they shall know them again. Verily it were a wonder if they did! After a year or two of such a fate, they might well be unrecognizable! One is almost ashamed of writing about such follies. The nirvana is grandeur contrasted with their heaven. The early Christians might now and then plague Paul with a foolish question, the answer to which plagues us to this day; but was there ever one of them doubted he was going to find his friends again? It is a mere form of Protean unbelief. They believe, they say, that God is love; but they cannot quite believe that he does not make the love in which we are most like him, either a mockery or a torture. Little would any promise of heaven be to me if I might not hope to say, 'I am sorry; forgive me; let what I did in anger or in coldness be nothing, in the name of God and Jesus!' Many such words will pass, many a self-humiliation have place. The man or woman who is not ready to confess, who is not ready to pour out a heartful of regrets—can such a one be an inheritor of the light? It is the joy of a true heart, of an heir of light, of a child of that God who loves an open soul—the joy of any man who hates the wrong the more because he has done it, to say, 'I was wrong; I am sorry.' Oh, the sweet winds of repentance and reconciliation and atonement, that will blow from garden to garden of God, in the tender twilights of his kingdom! Whatever the place be like, one thing is certain, that there will be endless, infinite atonement, ever-growing love. Certain too it is that whatever the divinely human heart desires, it shall not desire in vain. The light which is God, and which is our inheritance because we are the children of God, insures these things. For the heart which desires is made thus to desire. God is; let the earth be glad, and the heaven, and the heaven of heavens! Whatever a father can do to make his children blessed, that will God do for his children. Let us, then, live in continual expectation, looking for the good things that God will give to men, being their father and their everlasting saviour. If the things I have here come from him, and are so plainly but a beginning, shall I not take them as an earnest of the better to follow? How else can I regard them? For never, in the midst of the good things of this lovely world, have I felt quite at home in it. Never has it shown me things lovely or grand enough to satisfy me. It is not all I should like for a place to live in. It may be that my unsatisfaction comes from not having eyes open enough, or keen enough, to see and understand what he has given; but it matters little whether the cause lie in the world or in myself, both being incomplete: God is, and all is well. All that is needed to set the world right enough for me —and no empyrean heaven could be right for me without it—is, that I. care for God as he cares for me; that my will and desires keep time and harmony with his music; that I have no thought that springs from myself apart from him; that my individuality have the freedom that belongs to it as born of his individuality, and be in no slavery to my body, or my ancestry, or my prejudices, or any impulse whatever from region unknown; that I be free by obedience to the law of my being, the live and live-making will by which life is life, and my life is myself. What springs from myself and not from God, is evil; it is a perversion of something of God's. Whatever is not of faith is sin; it is a stream cut off—a stream that cuts itself off from its source, and thinks to run on without it. But light is my inheritance through him whose life is the light of men, to wake in them the life of their father in heaven. Loved be the Lord who in himself generated that life which is the light of men!

www.ingramcontent.com/pod-product-compliance
Lightning Source LLC
Chambersburg PA
CBHW032007230426
43672CB00010B/2276